Dear

He

book I wrote on my Childhood. I hope you enjoy it. I talk briefly in it of you & your

Hope you are well.

Love

rec'd Sept 21 - 2011

see p. 95 + 104

Barbie

B. Geraldine Meggait

Order this book online at www.trafford.com
or email orders@trafford.com

Most Trafford titles are also available at major online book retailers.

Printed in the United States of America.

ISBN: 978-1-4269-7606-3 (sc)
ISBN: 978-1-4269-7604-9 (e)

Library of Congress Control Number: 2011912358

Trafford rev. 07/27/2011

www.trafford.com

North America & international
toll-free: 1 888 232 4444 (USA & Canada)
phone: 250 383 6864 • fax: 812 355 4082

The Book Cover

The book cover was created and painted by granddaughter, Morgan Meggait. She was only fourteen years old when she agreed to take on the project and completed it soon after her fifteenth birthday. Morgan showed great talent and perseverance painting each dot on every leaf with exacting perfection. Thanks and good work, Morgan. Keep up the creativity!

DEDICATED TO

Martin
and each person in our
wonderful family

&

to family members who have graced
my life
but have now gone on to that greater life
with God:

My Mom & Dad,
Billy (my little Boy Blue),
Joyce, my childhood companion,
& Ginny who encouraged me to share my writing.

*YOU ARE ALL GREATLY LOVED AND
APPRECIATED!*

ACKNOWLEDGEMENTS

Special Thanks to:

- Shirley Campbell, writer-friend, who voluntarily edited *BARBIE,* using her expertise, and love of writing to help me.
- Son, Jim, who encouraged me to put down my memories into a book for family. Without him, my words would probably have remained unwritten forever.
- To Robin, Kathy, and Virginia, members of *Fellowship of the Pen,* who have encouraged me and listened to my rambling memories.
- To sister-in-law, Joan, for encouragement.
- To all my children, grandchildren, and birth family who loved me unconditionally.

Table of Contents

Introduction

Barbie is a true story, as true as memory is true. When memory failed, the author added details so the story would make sense. “Barbie” was the babyhood nickname of Barbara Geraldine (Gerry) Pouncy and was not used past babyhood except by her father and brother who called her “Barb.”

The author thinks of herself as Gerry or on formal occasions as Geraldine. By writing of *Barbie* she was able to look at her own life more objectively, as if she were a kindly older person looking at Barbie growing up with her accompanying joys and sorrows.

Most non-family names are fictitious. The story is filled with love, compassion, and understanding of a childhood and an era long gone.

Chapter One

Nestled in the Hills

The old woman sat in the lawn chair with her feet propped on the table built by her son Gordie. When she was sixty her eldest son, Jim, said to her, "Write. You have five good years left. You must write." She giggled. She had experienced many five years since then. Yet, his one request remained: "Write. I want you to write Barbie's story."

So here she sat, plotting the story. In it, she planned to call herself the "old woman" because she suspected that's the way other people viewed her. She would have been hurt or slightly annoyed if anyone else called her an "old woman." Or perhaps she might just laugh as she did when a friend referred to her as the "Ancient but Wise One." Just the same, she knew that on her next birthday less than three months away there would be eighty-two candles. That is, if anyone had the patience and courage to put them on the cake. Yet, she felt as young as ever, and in her mind she walked with the winds buffeting her body.

She gazed at her surroundings: the green grass of the field where cattle grazed and where fir, spruce, and pine trees of various hues graced her backyard. Then she picked up her pen.

Harry took one look at the red-faced, screaming mass of humanity and said, "Isn't she ugly?"

Verta cuddled their new baby closer. She knew the scrapes and bruises were just from the forceps and they'd disappear. When the baby quieted she said, "I'd like to call her Barbara. I just read a novel about this wonderful heroine named Barbara and that's what I want to call her."

The little girl knew her name. Her parents called her "Baby" and it sure sounded like Barbie to her. So Barbie it was.

Barbie was an active child who loved to run, jump, and climb the rafters in the barn. She also loved the hills that surrounded their little house in the picturesque Pembina Valley, Mowbray, Manitoba, that lay adjacent to the borders of North Dakota, U.S.A. She recalled when Daddy held her to look up towards the hills so she could see Santa as he rode through the skies on Christmas Eve. She thought she glimpsed him as he sped on his world-wide journey and knew she had to go to bed quickly so he could come to see her and little sister Joyce as they slept. He might leave some candy or a little treat in their stockings.

"Barbie, take care of Joyce while I make your birthday cake. You're going to be four tomorrow. There'll be candles on it and a penny wrapped in paper hidden in the cake. You girls will have lots of fun," said Mommy.

"Let's go see the ducks," Barbie said, as she took her sister's hand and led her outside.

They wandered towards the little pond walking on their tiptoes so they wouldn't frighten the wild ducks. They stood there hand-in-hand watching them swim and talk to each other in bird language.

"Let's go back to the house," said Barbie. "We'll see if Mommy has finished the cake." Sure enough, the cake was just going into the oven, and they watched as their mother put two more sticks of wood in the cook stove. "Come, girls," Mommy said. "It's time for your nap. Here's your dolly, Joyce."

Barbie knew that Joyce's dolly had been sent by Granny in England. Mommy had told her the story many times. The dolly was supposed to be for her own second birthday, but Barbie didn't want a doll. She wanted a horse instead. Mommy and Daddy couldn't change her mind, so on Christmas Eve they made a horse out of an old broom handle and some binder twine for a mane and tail. She had been so excited to see her rocking horse! She called him Charlie; "Chartie" was the way she pronounced it.

Even at four years old, Barbie still played with Charlie, her beloved and only toy. Barbie ran over to him, jumped on his back, and started to ride. In her imagination she was riding over the hills and far away.

The old woman sat in the passenger seat while her husband drove their car a couple of hours away for a doctor's appointment. The humming motor tempted her to sleep but she resisted, for the scenery looked beautiful. The hillsides that burned brown in deep summer were still pastel green. On the other side of the four-lane road lay the lake of many colors, whose waters shimmered with tints of blues, greens, and grays.

As she rode, the old woman compared the lack of medical help in her childhood to the medical system of the present day. Although people grumble and complain, she knew they were fortunate to live now. Her mind drifted to a place nearly half a country away to where Barbie lived when a child.

"Ah, a few quiet moments," said Verta. "Little Joyce and Barbie are both napping. I'll have time to start supper before they wake up. What on earth will I feed them?"

At that thought the old woman's attention drifted to the dilemma faced by Barbie's mother. She had no fridge to store food, no commercial cans to open so she could prepare a quick, easy meal, and no money to buy them even if available. Each morning her husband lowered a bucket of milk into a well of water to keep it cool. Of course, when she needed milk, the pail had to be raised again. The Great Depression had just begun and drought covered Southern Manitoba. How did Barbie's mother cope?

Verta had just started her supper preparations when she heard a piercing cry. Barbie was screaming. She ran to her. What could possibly be the matter?

"I can't move my leg, Mommy," she gasped between screams.

Verta checked Barbie over. "Polio!" she said. "Lots of people are sick with it." She remembered reading about Sister Kenney's treatment for polio patients: hot water compresses and lots of limb movement.

With no health care system available, Verta began the nursing process that lasted months. Slowly motion returned to Barbie's leg, but she walked with a limp, throwing her leg in an outward motion. Each time her leg returned, it hit and injured her ankle on the opposite side.

Ouch! A sick feeling developed in the pit of the old woman's stomach. She felt Barbie's pain and visualized the blood that tricked down her foot; and walking, falling, getting up, and trying again.

In November when Barbie was five, her mother went to the hospital. Nobody told Barbie why she had gone. But she remembered the day her Daddy took her and Joyce there to bring their mother home. The nurse walked with Mommy to the car. In her arms she carried a baby bundled in blankets. Mommy was carrying a bottle of cream soda. Joyce and big sister Barbie each had a little sip. It was red and tasted good. Another day Barbie's parents took her to a house that had been converted into an ice cream parlor. There she ate a dish of ice cream with a little wafer on the side. She never forgot those first, rare treats.

Why is it, the old woman mused, that Barbie remembered that sip of pop and a dish of ice cream but couldn't remember much about the new baby, or her jolly, huge grandfather who died that year. Kids have much to learn about what is important, but then maybe they are just easily satisfied with life.

The next morning the old woman rolled over in bed and opened one eye so she could see the clock: 4:55 a.m. Oh, no! It's too early. She had to go back to sleep. She closed her eyes and opened them again. Maybe it would help if she used the washroom and closed the curtains to block out the light. Just to sleep a little more. But no matter what steps she took, sleep would not come. The computer in her brain kept buzzing; conjuring up images of long ago and she couldn't find the off button. So, at six a.m. she walked downstairs and turned on the computer ready to write.

The slender, six-foot-tall, Englishman rose to sing. He looked like an aristocrat with his jet black straight hair, black mustache, a Roman nose and piercing dark brown eyes. At thirty-two years old Harry didn't feel young. He had gone to school at an early age, enlisted in the First World War when he was only fourteen, sailed on an ocean liner on two occasions to Canada, and now had a Canadian wife and three children. His beautiful tenor voice filled the hall as he sang an old English ballad.

"That's my Daddy," whispered Barbie to Mom as they sat in the audience listening.

Yes: Barbie's Daddy, thought the old woman. How can I ever describe him? It seemed to her that he must have been reared in a very strict, controlled environment with a stern but loving mother, and a father that seemed to be away from home a great deal lecturing about the life of Thomas Hardy and the Dorset countryside and entertaining audiences in various English locations. When the children finished their afternoon tea with their mother, Nanny would put Harry and his two brothers and one sister to bed for the night.

There were also the effects of his military training. She never knew if he saw action because he never discussed the war, although he was intensely patriotic. But she did know that once more he was being controlled, and the old woman suspected he had rebelled on numerous occasions. She had heard rumors that he went AWOL once to visit his very ill mother. Could he possibly have been the Black Sheep of the family? He left his family in England and came to Canada in 1923 for a short time, finally immigrating here in 1925. Did he not say to himself: "No longer will I allow others to dictate what I do or how I do it? I am now my own boss."

As she remembered his singing, the old woman could see how this handsome, charming gentleman had captured Verta's heart. Yet, deep down in her heart lay a fear that no one in the family could ever measure up to his standards.

Harry rose early and he and Verta milked the cows in the herd of fifty cattle while the children were still sleeping. Verta's hands were nimble and she milked many cows while he struggled to milk one or two. Life on their small acreage was much different from and harder than his life growing up in England. But he was under no one's authority, except of course the wind and the rain; the wind that blew the good soil off the land, and the rain that refused to come.

He carried the pails filled with milk into the house to put them through the cream separator, while Verta tended to the children who were now waking up. Harry loved both his children but he especially adored little Joyce. When he separated the milk from cream, she waited with a little tin cup held under the skim milk spout so she could catch the milk as it flowed out. As she drank cup after cup of the frothy, warm milk, she said, "I'm going to drink lots and lots so I can feed my babies from my stomach like Mrs. Johnson does."

Harry liked to watch Joyce in the winter time, as she dashed out in the snow almost up to her waist and then yelled, "Help! I'm ganglin'! I'm ganglin'." Harry didn't really know the word "ganglin'." His English was impeccable and grammatically correct, but Joyce made him happy and, besides, he was her Daddy so he helped her.

One day Harry and Verta couldn't find Joyce. They searched in all the usual places but she seemed to be nowhere. Barbie hunted too. She looked under one of the beds and up towards the bed-springs. There sound asleep, lay little sister between the springs and the feather tick that served as a mattress.

Besides being adorable, Joyce was also very sensitive. One day she and Barbie were playing together when a knock came at the door. Her mother opened it and there stood an old man and his wife. The woman's white whiskers intrigued Barbie, but Joyce took one whiff of the man and fainted. After the neighbours left, their parents explained to the girls that the man earned his money by trapping skunks. Some memories (and odours) last a long time.

The old woman woke from her afternoon nap, and now sat at the computer, occasionally taking a sip of tea. She didn't like sleeping in the daytime. It spoiled her night's sleep, but sometimes she just had to rest.

Yes, she remembered that Barbie and Joyce had been wonderful companions. Other friends were non-existent. They lived in a little world with no radio, television, and no extra money to buy treats. There was just Mommy, Daddy, and the three little girls.

On special occasions when Harry needed a break from the constant work, he went for a ride on his motorcycle—his very special possession. His brother who manufactured them in England had sent him one with a sidecar and their family name emblazoned on it.

Sometimes Harry took his whole family with him. Verta sat in the side car with baby Faith, and Joyce sat in front of Harry hanging tight to Barbie who sat in the front. Barbie enjoyed the wind blowing her hair and the feel of freedom as her daddy drove the bike.

Barbie thought it a special treat to visit Grandma Huston's house a few miles away. Her youngest aunt, Emily, was just starting her teen years.

"Come, Barbie," she said. "Let's go upstairs; your other aunts are dressing up. Let's watch them."

Together she and Emily walked upstairs. There Barbie saw amazing sights. Her aunts were putting things around their bare waists, things they called corselets. They were laced with flat strings that they pulled very tight.

Barbie stood there with wide eyes wondering why anyone would do that to themselves. They looked so uncomfortable. "That's the price of beauty," said Aunt Emily.

The old woman mused. She didn't recall Barbie's mother ever calling her daughters beautiful or even pretty. Yet, she supposed Verta thought they were cute with their hair cut in bangs; hair that reached to the tip of their ears and circled their heads. She sewed their little dresses and sometimes made them identical.

They looked like little stair steps, thought the old woman. She remembered their little sister, who would soon be a year old. Unlike her older sisters who had blue eyes, Faith's eyes were brown, large and somehow very knowing for one not yet walking.

One day, Verta decided to dress her three daughters in their best clothes and take them to visit some friends. While Harry hitched the horse to the buggy, she prepared the girls. Little Faith sat in the high chair ready and waiting to be carried outside, but there was one last thing Verta had to do before she left: use the toilet.

Telling the girls to be good, she went outside to the little structure sitting over a hole in the ground (commonly called the Out House or the Biffy). Toilet paper was whatever paper could be found—Eaton's catalogue if one was unlucky. It didn't do a good job and felt harsh to the bare skin.

Barbie was inside watching her little sister, who suddenly reached over to the nearby table, put her little hands in a pail of Golden Syrup and proceeded to smear it over her face and clothes just as her mother walked in the door.

Verta was not happy about delaying her plans while she washed and redressed little Faith.

The old woman lovingly remembered Barbie's gentle, patient mother. She recalled that Verta had been slightly annoyed when Faith pulled the syrup over herself, but she never yelled or spoke harshly. Barbie felt guilty. She knew that although only six, she was the eldest and therefore responsible for her little sisters when her parents weren't near.

It was about this time that Barbie thought she had learned the secret to becoming rich. Her front tooth had loosened. She wiggled and wiggled it until one day it fell out. Her mother told her that if she put the tooth in a glass of water something magical would happen to it. So she did and watched it all day but nothing happened. Next morning when she awoke she looked, and instead of the tooth, there sat a penny. The magic had happened.

That day as she explored their little farm she discovered an old cow's skull. She pulled and pulled to extract the teeth but they wouldn't budge. So she found an old basin and placed the whole skull in it, filled it up with water, and set it beside her bed.

When her mother discovered it she was dismayed, "But Barbie, the magic only works when it's your own teeth. Take this outside and throw it away." A disappointed Barbie obeyed and her dreams of riches died.

Barbie's sixth year, the old woman thought. That was the year she should have started grade one but didn't. She was still quite lame and would have had to walk one and a half miles to school and then the same distance home again. But in December her mother decided to take Barbie to a school Christmas concert as a gentle introduction to the place of learning.

It was a frosty December night when Verta hitched the horse to the cutter and bundled Barbie in warm clothing with a blanket tucked around her and a stone (warmed in the oven) at her feet. Then away they drove for a special mother-daughter evening of fun.

When they arrived at the little schoolhouse she hitched the horse to a rail with the others and led Barbie into the single room with desks of various sizes for grades one to eight. Some people sat in the desks while others stood in the aisles and around the edges of the room. Barbie watched and listened with amazement as the students entertained them. Then everyone started to sing, "Here comes Santa Claus! Here comes Santa Claus!"

Poor old Santa couldn't get in! The doorway was jammed with people so someone opened a window and he climbed through as everyone started to sing, "He's coming through the window!"

By the end of the program, Barbie was getting sleepy. Mother once more bundled her in outdoor clothing, hitched the horse and helped Barbie into the cutter. (The cutter was a small, light sleigh pulled by one horse. This one had a wooden roof and sides on it, with a door opening and a front window through which the driver controlled the horse with a set of reins.)

The road that led home was isolated, over a field and around a twisting lane to their little house nestled in the hills. All went well until something spooked the horse. He bolted and ran, breaking free of the cutter. Verta had wrapped the reins around her wrists several times and was pulled through the cutter-window.

Barbie woke suddenly. It was quiet and cold and her mother was gone! "Mommy, Mommy," she called repeatedly. Finally, Verta climbed back in the cutter and said, "It's okay, dear. Go back to sleep. The horse ran away but he'll run home and Daddy will come and find us." Mommy put her loving arms around Barbie and sang to her as she drifted back to sleep. Next thing Barbie knew she was safe in her own bed at home.

Barbie's poor mother, muttered the old woman. She suffered many years with that wrist. A tumor-like swelling developed on it. The doctor called it a ganglion and said he could not operate on it.

The winter of Barbie's sixth year passed in the little household, and now it was April; time for Barbie to go to school. The class was called grade A. It was only three months long and a precursor to grade one.

The first day, Mommy took Barbie to school and introduced her to the teacher. After that Barbie went alone even though the walk to and from school was torturous because of her lame leg, and by the time she got home she was tired, sore, and bleeding. But she did it. And school was lots of fun.

Barbie particularly noticed the boys. As yet, she had no brother and boys almost seemed to be different creatures; especially one boy named Jack. He seemed to be in mischief most of the time, and Teacher often reminded him to behave.

Verta had a problem. It was Barbie's first day at school and Joyce moped all day as she mourned for her playmate. Finally, Verta had an idea.

She hard-boiled several eggs, then coloured them with some vegetable dye. When Joyce was resting, Verta hid them outside in the empty rumble seat of an old wrecked car that sat under a tree in their yard.

After completing her task she went into the house and informed Joyce that the Easter bunny had hidden some eggs for her to find.

What fun Joyce had! And she jumped for joy when Barbie returned from school so she could show her where she had found the eggs. Barbie looked in the rumble seat but all she saw was a bunch of dirt and cobwebs. She found no sign of the Easter bunny's visit.

The old woman smiled gently at the memories. Oh, the joy children found back in those simple days, but always the joys seemed coupled with mother's love.

That was the summer of 1934, thought the old woman. The crops were drying up because of the drought and Barbie's father feared the cattle would starve. "We're moving," he said.

Harry never dawdled; once he made a decision he acted immediately. Their destination was Ochre River, a little village almost 200 miles to the north-west where Verta's mother had recently moved. The area was not as arid as the southern part of Manitoba.

Along with two teenagers, Harry's job was to drive his herd of fifty cattle along the roadsides until they reached their new location. The herd consisted of milking cows, heifers, steers, and young calves, and the bull. At one point a stray bull thought the herd looked interesting, hopped a fence and joined them.

The trip took almost two weeks. Along the way they milked the cows. They drank some of the milk. The rest was given away, or milked onto the sides of the roads.

"Hmm, I wonder how that worked for him," mumbled the old woman. Barbie's dad never communicated his fears or frustrations well, except for occasional curses. His swearing always seemed phony, coming from this man who spoke proper English.

At that the old woman's mind wandered to his wife. Life posed many problems for her, and no doubt this trip proved to be one of them.

Verta was eight months pregnant with three small children when her husband suddenly decided to move the family. In some ways, she looked forward to the change because she would be near her mother and she knew her mother would help her if necessary. Verta had married seven months after her seventeenth birthday. Now she was only twenty-six years old and life was incredibly complicated. She and her children were to be driven to their destination by an old neighbour in a rickety truck, carrying their meager belongings and a load of their furniture in the back.

During their travels, the truck broke down. They were stranded with no place to stay and nothing to eat while it was being repaired.

Never to be defeated by circumstances, Verta approached a hotel owner. "I'm desperate," she said. "I'll wash dishes for you if you'll give my children and me a place to stay till the truck is fixed, and some food to eat."

The hotel owner took one look at her swollen belly and her three priceless girls and said, "Why not? I have room and I could use someone to wash my dishes. You're hired. I'll show you your room."

"What fun!" said Barbie, as she led Joyce outside the hotel. By now they were tired of sitting crammed in the truck, and finally they could walk around and play. Baby Faith was sleeping and Mommy was washing dishes.

For a while Barbie and Joyce walked up and down the wooden sidewalks outside the hotel. The village was small, but to the girls it seemed big and exciting.

"I want to go back to Mommy," said Joyce.

"Okay," said Barbie, "I'll take you back."

Barbie looked up and down the street but all the buildings looked strange; as grown-up as she felt, she began to cry. Joyce looked at her and began to scream.

Actually, they were standing outside the hotel and their mother came to their aid. Putting her arms around them, she thought, "Will this trip never end?"

Next morning at breakfast Barbie and Joyce had their first taste of corn flakes. Joyce talked about them long after their bowls were empty and they were on their way to their new life.

Verta longed to be home in her mother's house. She hated being crammed in the truck's cab with the old man, the girls, and the unborn baby who kicked and struggled in her womb ready to pop out at any moment. Despite her discomfort she never complained. She was grateful for the ride.

But what lay ahead? No home. No money. No food. What would happen to her precious family?

Chapter Two

Life at Puddle Villa

The old woman put on her walking shoes, and with her stick tapping along she wandered out on the farm. She had a route that she took early sunny mornings. When she was young her stride was long and strong. She longed to walk as she once did, but now when she tried her chest hurt. So she slowed down to a comfortable pace.

Ah, yes; the story. It wasn't only Barbie's story. It was the story of many courageous and wonderful people.

Previous to driving the cattle, Harry had driven his motor bike to Ochre River. He stood surveying the countryside. There wasn't much from which to choose. Surely, his fifty dollars could buy a small bit of land.

He went to the local authorities. Yes, they had a quarter section of land. The municipality was trying to recover taxes from it. He could have it for the money in his pocket.

"I'll take it," said Harry.

Now along with his herd and his two traveling companions, Harry stood and surveyed his new purchase. There was no house or barns, and water stood in puddles on the ground. Well, at least there was rain to grow some crops. With that thought he dubbed his new home Puddle Villa.

He might have named it Rocky Villa, for rocks covered the land that stood at the foot of the Riding Mountains. Harry had never been afraid of hard work and he started to make plans.

First he corralled his cattle and started milking them. The separated cream could be sold for a small amount of money. He'd need every penny he could scrounge.

Next Harry cut some trees from the nearby mountain and borrowing a neighbour's mill, he sawed them into logs. He started to build a simple two-storey cabin. He had never learned carpentry but necessity was the mother of invention, or so the saying went.

Meantime Verta, the three girls, and his brand new baby boy were living with her mother as they waited for their new home to be completed.

"His new boy," Harry said to himself. "Girls were okay, but a son…now that was something to make a man proud." His wife had chosen the name Frank for him after her father but he nicknamed him Piccolo Pete; Pete for short.

"Back to work," said Harry, "time to think of my boy later."

"You girls go out to play and look after Faith. She might get lost in all the trees around here," said Verta to Barbie and Joyce.

Verta went inside and picked up the baby. Petie cried a lot. Milk didn't seem to agree with him and he wasn't gaining weight like her other children, but she adored her baby and tried to comfort him.

It was good to be home with her mother. Not a woman to demonstrate her love verbally, her Mom did it in practical ways. But then, Verta was practical too. Times were depressed and practicality was important for survival. It was uncommon to wonder, "What does my child think about this?" Instead she was thinking, "How do I keep my child alive" and "How can I possibly feed my family?"

Her mother's small house was crowded. Counting the baby who had died before delivery, she had birthed ten children. The two youngest still lived at home, as well as her elderly mother now called Grandma by everyone.

In her earlier years Grandma had been strict and bossy and thus never endeared herself to young Verta. Nevertheless, like other members of the family, Grandma had been spunky. When Verta and Harry had been courting, Grandma insisted on chaperoning them.

One day before they were married, Harry wanted to take his fiancée out for a car ride. Grandma went along. In order to frighten her, he drove fast around a plowed field. Grandma just held tight and yelled, "Is this the fastest this thing can go, young man? Faster! Faster!" No matter how hard he tried, Harry could not get rid of Grandma.

But now, a decade later Grandma had become senile. She was of slight build and still full of vim and vigour, but had lost much memory and judgment. Now while Verta and her mother busied themselves, Grandma slipped unnoticed outside to play with the children.

"Mommy, Mommy," said two-and-a-half year old Faith as she burst into the house. "Grandma and I had so much fun. I pulled Grandma in the wagon and she pulled me."

Verta looked at her daughter's smiling face, and then at Grandma's grin and knew that they had fun. When she quizzed Joyce and Barbie she discovered the whole story. The part that Faith had left out was that the wagon overturned, dumping Grandma and Faith in turn on the ground. They dusted themselves off, and laughed and then did it again and again!

One day soon after that, Grandma wandered from the house unnoticed, and when the family looked she could not be found. The terrain surrounding the house was mountainous and isolated. Neighbours were contacted and all came and searched. Finally, to everyone's delight, Grandma was located unharmed wandering around in the bush.

Barbie stood outside the new home their Daddy had built with the help of a few neighbours. She missed the Pembina Valley but loved the mountains near her new home. She looked at them and longed to be able to paint the view, but didn't know how.

The mountains were quite long, and she imagined that a giant animal had burrowed its way along the flat prairie leaving a pile of dirt behind it. Spruce, pine, and balsam trees grew on the mountain. Sometimes it looked green and sometimes blue. She knew the mountain range was called the Riding Mountains, and in her imagination she saw a horse and rider speeding across the top ridge. The mane and tail of the horse were flying in the wind, as the man hung tightly to the reins. She wished she could be on another horse riding along with them.

Barbie enjoyed playing with Joyce, and being with her other siblings.

Sometimes she rocked the baby. His skin looked pale, and his hair was coming in blonde. The baby often cried and when her daddy came in tired, she was afraid that he would be angry with him. Mother boiled barley water for him to drink because he vomited his milk. Barbie guessed that he wasn't feeling very well.

Like the baby, little Faith was cute. She sat in an old wooden high chair, and ate her supper. After she had finished eating, Faith continued to sit and suck on a crust of bread until she lulled herself to sleep. Occasionally, she would rouse to give another suck. She looked adorable with her black hair and big brown eyes. She was too young to play with Barbie, but her big sister loved her and baby Petie.

Soon September came and Barbie's father took her to school and introduced the teacher to her. When he said goodbye, he told her that she would have to walk home by herself as he and mother would be busy. That didn't frighten Barbie, for she used to walk to and from school in the Pembina Valley and she wasn't afraid to do it again even though it would be farther (two and one half miles to school, and the same distance home).

There were eight grades in this school, and Barbie looked at the grade four kids with admiration. They stood at the blackboard doing difficult long multiplication and division. Would she ever be as smart as they?

Her teacher's name was Mr. English. Every day all the grade one children were required to lay their crossed arms on their desks with their heads resting on them. After a while Mr. English said, "Time to wake up, children. Now, Barbara, what did you dream?"

"I didn't dream because I didn't go to sleep," said Barbie.

"But you have to dream, Barbara," said Mr. English. "Tell me what you dreamed."

"I didn't dream," said Barbie. Her teacher was silly. Had he not learned the difference between truth and a lie?

The old woman smiled. Barbie had been a child with a vivid imagination but she also had a strict moral conscience. If only he had said, "You can pretend, Barbara. That's okay." She hadn't meant to be stubborn.

Other activities at school were interesting though. Sometimes Teacher gave each of the children several coloured pegs. They looked like short, fat toothpicks (about 1/3 inch long) and with them the children made pictures: houses, roads, trees, or whatever their young minds imagined.

Each had one scribbler and pencil, and a reader. Barbie's mother had already taught her to read some. According to her Mom, Barbie learned to read when she was only four. The old woman smiled again. Barbie's mother was proud of her but the story was probably exaggerated. Nevertheless,

Barbie loved to read. It opened up a whole new world for her. Stories made up for her lack of friends and compensated for her limited physical abilities, although her leg was gradually getting better. She seldom fell, and no longer came home from school hurt and bleeding.

"Barbara," said Mr. English, "I am going to walk home with you today. I want to talk to your Mom and Dad."

"Okay," said Barbie, although she felt nervous. Why would her teacher want to talk to her father and mother? She hadn't been bad.

When they arrived at her house, she listened as Mr. English told her Mom and Dad that he suspected she had a problem seeing properly. Something could be wrong with her eyes. She seemed to have trouble reading the printing on the blackboard.

Barbie didn't think there was anything wrong with her eyes. They were better than other children's; she could see two cups when others could see only one. Actually, she could see two of lots of things. Other kids admired her for her skill.

Just the same she had to believe the adults. The words on the board didn't make sense at all. So, her parents made an appointment with an optometrist twenty-five miles away. When he examined her vision he said, "I think someone almost forgot to give you eyes when you were born. You are cute though. Your little nose reminds me of my pet bull dog." It took Barbie years to realize he was joking about both her eyes and her nose. She envisioned her nose as huge and flattened like that of a bull dog. Barbie was an adult before realizing that her nose was petite and not ugly at all. He did scare her into doing what he told her regarding her eyes though.

The doctor prescribed glasses and cotton batting stuffed behind the lens on Barbie's good eye. This made life very difficult and it was hard to see. Now it was more than her slightly lame leg that made her clumsy.

This was not Barbara's greatest worry, though; the glasses cost her parents fifteen dollars that they could not afford. The lens in the glasses for her bad eye had to be changed every six months and somehow the money was found. Her parents tried to ease her mind about the cost but she knew their burden. Barbie found a scrap of paper and added the expense every time her lenses were changed. She determined she would pay them back some day.

Little by little her sight improved. The leaves that had been a blur of green now became recognizable as individual leaves. Her sight was saved, although the vision in her left eye remained weaker than her right one.

The old woman sighed. Barbie never did repay her mother and father the money she owed. But how could a child ever repay her parents? It's impossible.

Winter came and the cold weather. When Barbie came downstairs for breakfast, she often stopped and looked at the windows. Her mother said that Jackie Frost came in the night and painted them. Of course, she knew Jackie Frost was pretend, but she loved the beautiful pictures that were created by the overnight frost and disappeared when her father lit the fire. Every morning it seemed that a new picture was painted.

Barbie stood and watched her mother work. Three flat irons sat on the stove. Her mother shoved wood into the stove to heat the irons; as they were heating Mom prepared a pad of cloth on the table and on it she put Barbie's dress. Then mother attached a handle to the iron and started her task. Soon the iron cooled and her mother exchanged it for a hot iron from the stove top.

"Oops," said Barbie as the handle of the iron gave way and the iron fell to the floor. Barbie watched her mother as she picked up the iron and carried on once more. Barbie saw the fear and frustration on her Mom's face and decided that at the first opportunity she would buy her mother a new handle that worked properly.

The local doctor was an interesting man. He never failed to help people whether or not they had money to pay him. Often patients insisted that he take something for his services and often gave him meat from their farm animals: a chicken, some pork or a quarter of beef. So as a sideline to his medical services he opened a butcher shop and sold his excess meat.

One day her parents took Barbie to visit the 'Doc' six miles away. The doctor examined her carefully and said, "She's underweight. I don't know why. I'd like to have her stay with my wife and me for a week and I'll observe her."

So Barbie went to live with the doctor and his wife, a nurse. At meal times they served foods that she had never seen. One day the nurse served stewed tomatoes. "I think they're poison," Barbie said to herself while out loud she said, "No, thanks."

When Barbie had free time, she was allowed to walk around the village. She had a mission. Her parents had given her the large sum of twenty-five cents to spend any way she chose. To Barbie this amount seemed like a fortune. Surely she could find an iron handle for her mother. But although she searched in the stores she couldn't locate one.

At week's end, Barbie was sent home with no diagnosis from the doctor. She returned to their meager food supply and her picky eating habits. They had lots of milk but she didn't like it. Sometimes it tasted terrible after the cows had eaten some weeds. At one time she had enjoyed ice cream but one day at a community picnic the homemade ice cream made her very sick, so now she didn't even eat ice cream, or the gummy oatmeal porridge that her mother made every morning. Barbie liked mother's home-made cheese though. The rare treat proved so popular that it was eaten before it had a chance to age!

The old woman rose from bed and looked outside. The skies were overcast and she could smell rain in the air. "Does one smell rain?" she wondered. Oh, well, maybe she didn't smell rain but some sense enabled her to realize that rain was coming today.

For many days the sun beat down upon the people in the Okanagan and the old woman felt as if she were living in an oven. Ah, for a drop of rain and some cooling breezes.

Still she loved the world. Last night she had stood by the window before retiring and whispered, "Thank you for the beauty of the earth, and the glory of the skies." The sky looked splendid, as stray clouds caught the rays of the setting sun in hues of reds, blues, and grays. She remembered that as a little girl, Barbie had always loved the clouds.

Summertime came to Puddle Villa and although she loved school, Barbie enjoyed the days off. She had few playmates except her sisters and no toys, so she improvised. Today Barbie felt like taking a stroll.

She walked outside and climbed on a tall stack of loosely piled hay. She lay on it, gazing at the sky and the billowy clouds as they rolled across the heavens. As she looked, Barbie marvelled at the wondrous castles and flying angels that appeared in various shapes and sizes.

After a while she climbed down to return to the house and see if her mother needed her. Suddenly, she realized that one of her shoes was missing. "*Daddy will kill me*!" she thought. With rising panic, she searched and searched but failed to find the lost shoe. She closed her eyes tight and prayed, "Dear God, help me to find my shoe. Amen." She opened her eyes and there in plain sight was her shoe.

Barbie learned all about praying from her mother. Her granny from England had sent her a Bible for her first birthday. Barbie's mom was the guardian of the Bible. She placed it high in the kitchen cupboard, out of the reach of little hands that would destroy its pages. Then on special occasions mother took the Bible down and read a short story to the girls.

The old woman paused in her story. Memories seemed to invade her mind: all the girls crowded round Barbie's mother while she sang to them, recited long poems often telling sad stories, or read the Bible. How the old woman wished Barbie still had the book, but through the years it had been used frequently and then destroyed.

They didn't have many other books. Granny sent them some of the adventures of Peter Rabbit and Mr. McGregor by Beatrix Potter. They loved hearing the stories and looking at the pictures in the books.

Although the children never met Granny, they looked forward to her letters from faraway England. Whenever one of them had a birthday, Granny sent five pounds (then worth about $25) to spend on the birthday-child. When their mother received the money, she sent to Eaton's catalogue for cotton fabric. Birthdays were spaced throughout the year, and Barbie's mother was able to dress her children in simple but good clothes all year. No money remained for party dresses, though.

The children gathered around as they watched their parents open a big box sent from England. They had never seen a big parcel like that before. The girls' excitement grew as they watched Mom and Dad pull out dresses that their cousins had outgrown. "Yippee!" said Barbie as she tried on a shiny taffeta dress that fit her perfectly. "I'm gonna wear it to school Friday night for the Christmas concert."

At the concert the teacher lined the children on stage to sing for their parents. They stood straight and proud and sang: "You better be good, you better not cry; you better not pout I'm telling you why. Santa Claus is coming to town." Suddenly, Barbie felt the first sign of trouble. *Rip. Rip. Rip.* The taffeta dress had deteriorated as it sat for years in a trunk. The audience never noticed, but Barbie's face reddened.

Somehow Barbie survived the evening, and now they were getting into an old canvas-topped car that her father had acquired.

The country road was crowded with slow-moving vehicles and Barbie's father decided to pass the one ahead of them. As he did, he saw in his headlights a boy sitting in a sled pulled by a dog. To avoid hitting the child, Barbie's Dad swerved hard and the car landed on its side in the left ditch.

The car came to an abrupt stop. Barbie sat there stunned and then heard her mother calling: "Barbie, are you okay?"

"Yes, Mommy," Barbie said.

Faith was busy chattering to her mother, and Verta held baby in her arms but she couldn't account for Joyce.

"Joyce, are you all right?" No answer. "Joyce, are you all right?" Again and again Verta's panicked voice called out her name, but there was no answer.

Finally, in the dark of the night, her father found Joyce. She had crawled safely through a hole in the car's canvas roof and did not hear her mother's calls.

The old woman remembered that night well. It had been a night of intense embarrassment and near disaster, but somehow Barbie's family survived. As Barbie's practical mother often said, "Never cry over spilled milk."

That was the only adventure she recalled for the family in that car. Perhaps it became a relic as many cars did in the dark, depressed era of life in Manitoba during the 1930s. Or maybe someone turned it into a Bennett buggy to be pulled by horses, rather than run by gas that no one could afford.

Still, the old woman thought, Barbie never seemed to feel deprived, nor did she act as is if she were poor. She only remembered that Barbie felt sorry for the "poor children." Tears trickled down Barbie's cheeks as she talked of a family who lived in a one-room cabin. The floor was built of boards, and the cold, bitter, winter air crept through the cracks. Barbie wondered how the parents were able to keep those children warm, let alone fed.

The old woman remembered the valiant efforts of Barbie's parents. She understood why the children walked barefoot during summer holidays, and why Barbie's father would be furious if he discovered that Barbie had lost her shoe. Years later when Harry returned to the site of Puddle Villa he found a shoe he had made out of pieces of an old tire. Such dreadful poverty, thought the old woman; yet Barbie never seemed to mind walking in bare feet. She loved the feel of the prairie grasses as they tickled her toes, except for that awful day when she cut her foot.

Daddy was out in the field mowing hay, and Barbie and Joyce decided to take a walk and watch him work. Their bare feet felt the dirt, grass, and weeds as they walked the quarter mile to where their Dad was working. He never noticed them as they walked through the tall grass.

Barbie's scream echoed in the mountains as blood gushed out, yet busy and preoccupied her dad did not hear. She had stepped on the jagged edges of a quart jar, broken in half. Hollering at the top of her lungs, she limped back to the house. Her mother bathed her wound and wrapped her heel in clean cloths, while Joyce looked on in horror. In time the wound healed, but Barbie always carried a scar on the heel of her left foot.

The old woman remembered that summer. It soon fled on the wings of time, as summers always seem to do. In September Joyce started school and the two little girls walked together.

As Joyce walked along beside Barbie, she glanced at the bushes that grew along each side of the dirt road. She said, "Are there any bears in the bush?"

"No, of course not," said Barbie. "They're all in the mountain."

"But I'm scared," said Joyce.

As the girls walked, Joyce kept talking about bears. Barbie glanced furtively up and down the road.

"Something is coming," said Barbie.

"Bears!" said Joyce, and they began to run.

Every so often they looked back but the bears seemed to be gaining ground. Finally, they reached a clearing. It was a farmer's field. They ducked under the barbed wire fence and kitty-cornered across the field to the schoolhouse across the road. Panting and exhausted, they flopped in their desks.

Several minutes later, two classmates came in puffing and out of breath. "What's wrong with you two? We tried to catch up with you to walk to school together but you kept running."

Joyce never feared cars until one day. She and Barbie were walking home from school. Joyce walked on the left-hand side of the road, while Barbie walked on the right side. Usually the road was quiet with no vehicular traffic but suddenly a car came along behind them. Without warning, Joyce darted across the road to be near big sister.

The car stopped and the driver yelled and swore at Joyce, who huddled close to Barbie. When they arrived home, Barbie repeated to her mother each word that the stranger had said to Joyce. Barbie had never said terrible words like those before and she felt guilty. She decided that never again would she swear even when repeating someone else.

A few months later, Barbie and Joyce had another adventure when walking home. Rain had swollen and overflowed the banks of the river that usually wandered lazily along. When Barbie and Joyce rounded the corner about a quarter mile from the schoolhouse, they could not see the road or the deep ditches that lay along each side. More than two miles away their parents had no idea their children were in danger.

Hand in hand, Barbie and Joyce stood wondering what to do. Then they noticed a farmer coming with his horse and wagon. The farmer drove across the waters, told the children to climb on, and soon they were safely out of the flooded area and continued to walk home.

How Barbie's parents must have worried about the girls, thought the old lady. In winter they wore dresses covered by coats that never stopped the wind. A knit scarf was pulled around their necks and sometimes over their heads, as the prairie winds blew in the sub-zero weather. Woollen mittens covered their hands. They had on cotton stockings held up by garters, and rubber boots pulled over their shoes. Years later her Dad apologized to Barbie for sending her to school in dangerously cold weather, but Barbie shrugged off the apology. It was just life: sometimes difficult; sometimes full of fun.

But life would get more difficult for the little family who lived at Puddle Villa, and the old woman sighed as she remembered.

Chapter Three

Just Family

The Okanagan Valley had been hot, and the old woman had stayed indoors to remain cool. The family home that her husband, Martin, had inherited from his parents stayed comfortable on the main floor. But today light-gray clouds blanketed the morning sky; thus shielded from the sun she decided to take a walk. She grabbed her walking stick and opened the gate, then walked past the chirping marmot on the woodpile. As she went up the farm road towards the mountain, she met her husband carrying a heavy piece of irrigation equipment. She knew it was too heavy for him; although he was eighty-two years he refused to slow down.

Blondie, the Siamese cat, meowed and the old woman waited for it to catch up to her. Together she and the cat meandered towards the dry creek. Partway there she looked back. Blondie's attention had been diverted, so the old woman walked on alone.

A tiny chipmunk sat on a rock, curious about this human, but as the old woman neared it fled to safety behind the rock.

Soon the walk ended and the old woman sat in front of her computer. She needed to write. Barbie's story was bursting to continue, but where should she start?

The family were all sitting around the table in the main downstairs room. To the east a lean-to kitchen had been added to their Puddle Villa home, and all the family slept in the upstairs bedroom. But now they were ready to eat supper. The children ate in silence for their father's edict was, "Children should be seen and not heard."

They tried very hard to please their father, except when it came to eating the crusts off the homemade bread. Without drawing any attention to their actions, Barbie and Joyce placed their crusts on a ledge that ran under the table. Their Dad never saw.

The old woman smiled. Years later Barbie's mother confessed that she gave the crusts to the chickens and her husband never found out. If he had, the girls would have been in trouble. When they were naughty, Dad would point to the stairs and say, "Bed. No supper." Later on, their mother would bring them some pepper broth (a concoction of pieces of bread with hot water poured over them and drained off. To that she would add bits of butter and salt and pepper) or the bowl might contain bread and cold milk with brown sugar on top. She remembered that when guests joined the family, the children were required to eat after the grownups finished their meal. The old woman knew that being a kid at Puddle Villa wasn't always fun.

Barbie and Joyce waited for their father to return from town. Every week he took his cream can to the train station to be shipped. Once a month he went to the little corner post office where a letter with a small cheque in it waited for him. With the money he would buy a few groceries. Sometimes, the storekeeper would give him a little bag of hard candies. When he came home each child would get one to suck on; that is, if he considered them to be "good." Sometimes little Faith rebelled at his sternness. "You can keep your stinking old candy. I don't want any."

One day their Dad came home excited. "Look," he said to their mother. "I bought an unbreakable lamp chimney. The storekeeper threw it across the room and it didn't break."

Later that week, a neighbour dropped in. "Look what I bought," said Harry, as he picked it up and threw it across the room. He watched in disbelief as it smashed in millions of tiny pieces.

Verta stared in dismay. Lamp chimneys cost money and were precious. Sometimes she was almost overwhelmed by Harry's rash behaviour. In those pre-electricity days lamp-bases were filled with kerosene, sometimes called coal oil. A wick then led to the chamber above where it was lit and burned with a flickering, dim light. With its light Verta sewed or mended clothing, or did a little reading. Next morning when she washed the dishes she also washed the lamp chimneys, for smoke darkened the glass chimney each evening.

In the evening after the children were put to bed and the cows were milked, Harry sometimes put on the radio and he and Verta listened. They didn't use the radio much because it was battery-powered and would lose strength if overused, and of course batteries cost money.

Once in a while, Barbie and Joyce were allowed to get out of bed with their nightgowns on, and listen to the Old Barn Dance with Lulu Belle and Scottie. The whole family enjoyed the lively music.

The old woman smiled. It was a simple age with simple pleasures. She recalled watching Barbie's mother tap dance, as her Irish blue eyes sparkled with joy and her short hair bobbed up and down in time to the music.

Often the children gathered around their mother before bedtime as she sang, or recited poem after poem. Many of them were sad, but the children didn't mind.

"Tell us again," Barbie said, "about Little Boy Blue who died and left his toys behind." The children listened with rapt attention.

The old woman stopped her writing and looked off into the distance. She had first understood the sadness of this story when her own Little Boy Blue left his toys behind many years later. But Barbie only thought of the patient toys.

Then Joyce asked their mother to sing the song called the Mistletoe Bough. It was another sad story about a group of boys and girls who were playing hide and seek during the Christmas festivities. One little girl hid in a trunk and was never found again. Then mother sang them the song about the little Gypsy Boy who died alone at the close of the day. So many sad stories, but they were never scary. They were of other children, and Mother kept them safe.

Their mother recited many poems that she had memorized in school. Joyce's favourite one started:

"I wish, how I wish,
That I had a little house;
With a mat for the cat
And a holey for the mouse."

The poem continued telling about this wonderful little house. All Joyce wanted to do in life was to be a mother with a dozen children and have a little house "with a clock that goes tock in the middle of the room, and a kettle and a cupboard and a big birch broom." Joyce wanted to have a house that she could clean and clean until it "sparkled like a bright new pin," just as the poem described.

After story time, mother helped the older children say their little prayers:

Gentle Jesus, meek and mild,
Look upon this little child;
Pity my simplicity,
Suffer me to come to Thee. Amen

Barbie didn't understand "Pity my simplicity" but she loved the "Gentle Jesus, meek and mild" and she wanted to be just like him. After prayers, Verta put the children to bed with a kiss and said, “Good night” then walked out to the barn to help Harry milk the cows.

Barbie, Joyce, Faith, and little Petie were sound asleep in their beds when suddenly the girls awoke and smelled smoke.

“Mommy, Daddy,” they called again and again. There was no answer. Their parents were out milking.

The girls knew how dangerous fire could be. Barbie remembered when she had smelled smoke before. That time they were sitting at the supper table when the room became smoky. Daddy looked up the stairway to where the stovepipe went through a hole in the ceiling. “Quick, get me a pail of water,” he said to Verta. Then he ran upstairs to try to smother the fire with blankets and the water Verta quickly brought him.

But now fear overcame Barbie and Joyce and they pulled the feather ticks over their heads. Faith, not quite four years old, climbed out of bed. “I’m not scared,” she said, “I’m going to get Mommy and Daddy.”

She ran down the stairs in her nighty and bare feet, across the ice and snow to the barn and warned her parents. They immediately fixed the smoky stove, put Faith back to bed and reassured the children.

It was a desperate age, mused the old woman. She remembered well how Barbie’s father cursed the land, the cold, the poverty, and how her mother quietly gentled the children who huddled round her, like chicks under a mother hen. Despite his strong opinions, Barbie’s father had a hard time supplying for his family, but he persisted. He had a work ethic and a persistence that carried them through many difficult years, and the old woman admired those qualities in him.

Harry's agile mind worked day and night conjuring up ways to improve his farm. One day he was busy forging some pieces of iron outside on an open fire pit, when out toddled little year-old Petie. Seeing his Daddy across from him, he walked right onto the hot embers. Once more Verta heard the scream of a child. She ran outdoors grabbed her little son, and seeing a pail of cold lard sitting nearby she plunged both his feet into it.

The old woman shivered. Doctors would be angry at this first aid treatment today. Yet back in that era, people did what they knew and what they could, and little Petie recovered without a doctor's help. She thought his parents were amazing. They toiled endlessly and did whatever they could to keep their family alive and healthy.

Harry was busy outside, cleaning the barns, mowing or stacking hay; whatever task the day demanded. Verta had lots to do with a husband and four children for which to care, besides the daily milking, washing the separator parts, fuelling the lamps and washing the lamp-chimneys every day, and a million other jobs. She was not quite twenty-eight years old. Her fine features showed only a hint of the hard work and stress she was experiencing. An inch streak of white hair was combed back and added a certain charm to the salt and pepper look of the rest of her dark brown hair.

Verta pushed back a stray strand as it fell across her forehead. Today she was baking bread. The house felt hot and she was tired, but her family had to eat so she stoked the wood stove with more sticks of wood. She liked the feel of kneading bread and her hands were nimble and adept.

Her week had been busy. Monday she heated big tubs of water on the stove, and then moved them on to a small table. The clothes stood ready in piles of whites, colours, and dark work clothes. Then she took up each individual article (starting with the white ones; the darkest came last) and putting soap on it she rubbed it vigorously on a portable scrub board. When the clothes were washed, she got fresh warm water and rinsed the soap out of them. When all was finished, she hung them on the clothes line with wooden pegs. Later in the day when the clothes had dried, she brought them in and put them in piles ready to be ironed the next day.

Wednesday she had to turn cream into butter. The girls liked to watch her whenever possible. The ladle went up and down in the churn until butter-lumps formed. Verta then washed the butter several times in cold water to rinse out the whey, salted it, and formed it into blocks using a wooden form.

Ah, sighed, the old woman, readers will be weary as they imagine all that work. People named those years "the dirty thirties" and life was grim as starvation loomed around each corner. Women had to scrub floors, wash dirty faces, bandage cuts, and cook meals. Work seemed never-ending. There were no automatic fridges, washer and driers, dishwashing machines and all the modern conveniences. Of course, no one had a phone to answer. Usually, no knocks came to the door. Everyone was busy surviving.

The old woman looked around her house at all the toys she had for her great-grandchildren. One of her grandchildren said, "Grandma, you should throw out these old toys and buy some new ones." However, buying new toys never became her priority. Back during Barbie's childhood, toys were almost non-existent; no one had the money to buy them and no time to make any. Children learned to be independent and creative.

Of course, reasoned the old woman, independence and creativity can be developed in many ways and many modern toys do a great job. Many paths lead to the same outcome.

"You can go outside to play, Barbie," her Mom said. So Barbie walked outside. Once or twice in her life she had played *Red Light, Green Light*, or *Anti-I-Over the Woodshed*, but there weren't enough kids to play those games; anyway the only game she liked to play was *school*. She determined to become a teacher when she grew up. She tried to coax Joyce and Faith to be students and sit still while she taught them. But no, they had other ideas. Each of her sisters owned one special doll and they didn't want to sit still while big, bossy sister taught them. So Barbie had to improvise. She stuck sticks of wood into rows of soft earth and proceeded to teach. She was getting ready for grown-up life and she knew exactly what she wanted to do.

Barbie felt her stomach growl, knew it was almost time for supper and went inside. Joyce and Faith were already in the house asking for food. Mother was peeling potatoes for soup and she gave each child a piece of raw potato with salt sprinkled on it. The soup was mostly made of boiled, mashed and salted potatoes, accompanied by lots of homemade bread and butter.

The old woman thought, I guess that's why many of the relatives developed Type Two diabetes; when children they ate too many carbohydrates. The doctor said it was because so many of their Irish ancestors drank whiskey. It could have been that too, although Verta determined that her family would not go that route. The old woman never saw either Verta or Harry drink alcohol, although Harry smoked cigarettes.

Barbie, Joyce, Faith, and little Petie all tried to stay out of their Dad's way. He was very cranky. They had heard him tell Mom that he was quitting smoking; it cost too much. So he quit, but every day he became crankier and crankier. Barbie prayed, "Dear God, make Daddy start smoking again. Amen."

Barbie didn't know what she was asking, the old woman thought. Their father started smoking again, but she doubted that God had anything to do with his decision. Years later he did stop though, and by then Barbie was happy for him. The old woman hung her head with sadness. The children were desperately afraid of their father; yet she knew he loved them. During his rare good mood he had lots of fun playing with them, but the children often forgot about those times; most of the time he was tense and cranky. And that's what they remembered.

All the children gathered around their Dad and Mom who had just woken. Mommy had brought Daddy his breakfast in bed. This was a special treat for him and the cows could wait for a few minutes. When he finished eating, the children climbed all over him while he told them the story of Jack and the Beanstalk. When he impersonated the giant Daddy roared, and as little Jack he became very quiet. The children loved to watch his face screwed in grimaces as he mimicked the giant; "Fe, Fi, Fo, Fum, I smell the blood of an Englishmun'. Be he alive or be he dead, I'll grind his bones to make my bread!" Too soon playtime was over and he said, "That's it. Go get dressed. I have to milk the cows."

Occasionally Daddy brought in the wash tub and set it in the middle of the kitchen, while Mommy poured some warm water in it. It was bath time. First, little Petie had a bath, next Faith, then Joyce, (sometimes Daddy called her Jock) and finally Barbie. Barbie thought she was getting too old for this kind of thing and asked her mother to put up a big towel in front so nobody could see her.

The old woman remembered Barbie's embarrassment. But how else were her parents to bathe the children? No one they knew had running water, a bathtub, or indoor toilets. If rich people had them, they certainly didn't know about it—they hadn't heard of such luxuries. Every day they washed themselves, and their mother always checked to see if they washed their elbows or behind their ears (lots of kids forgot). Sometimes they washed all over with a sponge bath using a basin of warm water. It wasn't as thorough as a tub bath, but it was better than a casual wash.

A pattern of life had been established at Puddle Villa and Barbie assumed that life would last just like it forever, but forever is a long time and at Puddle Villa things would take a drastic and scary turn.

Chapter Four

DARK DAYS AHEAD

The old woman walked to the window and pulled back the curtain. She wished to see outside before she crawled into bed for the night.

Tall trees silhouetted the darkening night sky as gray clouds inched across the west, and behind all lay the mountains that she loved.

"Gorgeous," said the old woman, "and tomorrow I must write of the dark night at Puddle Villa, and the family who walk silhouetted through the memories of my mind."

Verta's day started like thousands of others: minding the children, doing chores, and preparing meals. Just days before, she and Harry had listened with concern to the radio about the abdication of King Edward V111 of England. Her husband's love for the "Old Country" was evident, but Verta had no time to think of that now. Much work remained before she could say "Good night," and climb into bed.

Suddenly, the door opened and Miles Christian yelled, "Harry's been hurt! We're taking him in the sleigh to the hospital."

He said no more and took off.

Verta stood dazed, uncertain what to do next. The hospital was twenty-six miles away, and she had no vehicle to follow her husband. Besides, she needed to care for the children and feed the cattle.

Harry had left the house in the morning, as he had done every day this week, to go to the neighbour's place and help the men saw some logs with a little mill. Snow lay on the ground and Verta had already been planning Christmas celebrations. "What next?" Verta thought. "How could things get any worse?"

Until the accident Harry had experienced a normal day. He was glad to be able to work and get his share of the logs, for much building remained to be done at Puddle Villa. He put his foot on the base of the mill to steady himself. His leg slipped on the icy surface and fell into the whirling saw blade.

Soon Harry realized he was lying on a sleigh as he drifted in and out of consciousness. He felt the icy cold of blood on his leg and knew that he would die if the bleeding didn't stop. He struggled to sit up and muttered, "Tourniquet…tourniquet."

The men looked at him trying to understand him as he struggled to show them how to stop the flow of blood. Then he fell back as weakness overwhelmed him.

One of the neighbours in the sleigh said, "Let's drive him to old man Wilson's. He's got a car. We have to get Harry to the hospital before he dies on us."

Harry next became aware as the men carried him into the hospital, and grave-faced medical staff examined his leg.

Back in the neighbourhood, word of the accident spread and people came to help Verta. By now Grandma had moved and Faith travelled with Aunt Emily to her grandmother's place in the northerly town of Flin Flon, Joyce stayed at some neighbours, while Barbie went to stay with her Great-aunt Alice. Verta remained at home with baby Petie and all the chores.

"Now you be good, or I'll have to use my paddling machine on you."

Barbie stared at her aunt as she spoke those words. She knew paddling meant a spanking, but what was a paddling machine? She was frightened. Barbie didn't know her grandmother's sister. She looked old and had white hair. As Barbie walked through various rooms in the house she searched for anything that might look like a machine used to spank kids.

Finally, Barbie saw a machine that she had never seen before. That must be it. Later when her aunt spun some wool into yarn she learned its name. It was called a spinning machine, and she stopped worrying.

Nevertheless, Barbie was determined to be good; although, in truth, she was too frightened to be anything but good. One night her aunt had company. At supper time

Barbie along with her aunt and guests sat at the big table ready to eat. Barbie was on her best behaviour, and when the potatoes came to her she politely offered them to the person sitting beside her. The potatoes never did return to her. "Sometimes it's really hard to be good," she thought.

Time passed and now it was Christmas Eve, and she laid one of her stockings besides her bed so Santa could fill it. The next morning she awoke and picked up her stocking. As she hoped there were a few candies and an orange in her stocking, but unexpectedly an onion was in the toe. She knew who put it there; her silly uncle Bus who was also living with her great-aunt. And although there were no toys, her uncle helped her through that scary time with his constant teasing.

The old woman sat beside the computer and rubbed her face. It had been a hot summer day and the house was sweltering. She walked outside, picked up her walking stick, and wandered off over the farm. She passed the cattle feeders, her daughter-in-law's pretty flower garden, and beside the hayfield, as Fergus the border collie danced at her side.

Steel gray clouds darkened the evening sky, with streaks of rain and flashes of lightning to the north and west. A cooling breeze blew her hair as her stick tapped its way over the ground. The old woman didn't need the stick for walking, but she liked the feel of it in her hands. As she walked she reminisced about those days long ago when troubles assailed Barbie's family. She knew that thunder clouds always blew away and just like them the family's pain would dissipate.

Verta's family were almost all home. Although the hospital had released Harry, they warned him that he might not survive the injury. If he did, he might never walk again.

Barbie and Joyce were both home. It was good to have their help minding little Petie. However, Faith was still with Grandmother and Aunt Emily who still lived with her. Verta would be happy when she had her last child home safely, but whatever would she do without Harry's help? Never one to be beaten by circumstances Verta started to think about her situation. Harry's illness and their isolation were both threats to her family's safety.

One day her loneliness lifted as she greeted visitors. They were travelling missionaries from the Anglican Church. Verta welcomed them. She had a longing in her heart for God, and to talk to others about him. They gave Verta some literature but too soon they left.

Barbie was glad to be home with Mommy and Daddy, although she had come to realize that her stern-looking aunt was really kind; still home was better.

She walked outside and gazed at her beloved mountains, and around the yard. Everything looked the same, but things were different inside the house. When Daddy came home from the hospital he was either in bed or sitting in a big chair with a warm blanket around him.

Barbie helped her Mom all she could but she was busy with school. She and Joyce left home early in the morning because of the long walk, and it was almost suppertime when they got home.

Soon Daddy was feeling a bit better but he still couldn't work. When Barbie got home from school, her father always seemed to be busy doing something with his hands. He made a monkey that climbed a string, and the first game of Dirty Marbles Barbie had ever seen. Later she learned that most people called it Chinese Checkers. Oh course, the games were for the grown-ups. Children could just watch and not touch. They liked looking at the game though. Sometimes Barbie noticed that he was knitting.

One day Barbie came home from school and Aunt Emily was visiting. She had brought Faith home. Barbie and Joyce looked longingly at all the pretty new dresses that her aunts had given their little sister.

The old woman remembered Barbie's adorable little sister. Somehow Barbie and Joyce had been a bit jealous of their aunt's special treatment of her. Many years later, Faith still bears a regal appearance as if the special treatment as a child bestowed a special blessing on her.

Although Verta worked day and night, food was getting scarce. All her baking supplies were gone. All that remained were some potatoes. Just the same, when a knock came to the door she smiled at the men who stood there and asked them in. The afternoon wore on and the men didn't leave. Finally, the children began to ask for their suppers. So Verta peeled the potatoes and set them on the stove to boil. When they were ready she set the table and said: "Please join us for supper." One of the men spoke for the group and said, "Thank you. We'd like to." Then she served them the meal of mashed potatoes.

The next day the men came back with 100 pounds of flour, 100 pounds of oatmeal, and 100 pounds of sugar. The little family was safe for the time being. It was the only time throughout the depression years that they received any social assistance. It was an era of dogged pride and personal independence.

Verta's mind was made up and she spoke with unusual authority to her husband, "Harry, if you're not going to get well, I am not staying on this farm alone with all this work. We're selling."

Winter still gripped Manitoba when Verta made this decision. On frosty nights as she milked the cows, she could hear the eerie whistle of the steam train six miles away in the little village. It was a lonely sound and matched her spirit.

So they sold the farm and set the date of April 15th for the sale of the farm animals and equipment.

Faith watched the sale as she held close her little black dolly, Patsy, while Barbie's job was to watch Petie so that he wouldn't become hurt or get in anyone's way.

Joyce felt important and grown up. The sale was on her birthday and she was now eight years old. She enjoyed all the people who had come to buy things. "Today's my birthday," she proudly announced to any who would listen. Many of them gave her a penny or two, and sometimes even a nickel. "I'm getting rich," she said to Barbie. "I wonder what I should buy with all this money, or maybe I should save it."

She probably saved it, the old woman thought. Joyce had great self-control, even as an adult; the old woman smiled as she thought about Barbie's childhood companion. What a unique and special sister and friend she had been to Barbie.

Barbie stood with Joyce as they looked at their new home, while Faith and Petie ran around exploring. Their parents had bought a small piece of land on the outskirts of a little village named Ochre River, Manitoba, with a population of about 250. They bought it from an old man who said he would move out before occupation day, but when they arrived with their meager household belongings and the children, he was still living in the house. After some discussion with the old man, Mr. Sullivan, it was agreed that they would move into the back of the house while Mr. Sullivan lived in the front until he found another home.

Verta was frustrated in their cramped quarters with four little children. She tried to keep the children playing outside in the daytime, but at night they made normal children sounds. Mr. Sullivan frequently yelled, "Shut those brats up!"

Other problems cropped up as well. One day, Faith went to use the "potty" (little children didn't have to use the outdoor toilet). "Mommy, there's a bedbug in the potty," she yelled in a loud voice. "Shh," Verta said as she looked out the window to see if any neighbours were close enough to hear. *As soon as Mr Sullivan moved she planned to fumigate those bugs.*

Finally, Mr. Sullivan moved out; Verta got rid of the tenacious bugs, and family-life improved.

Barbie enjoyed the new surroundings although they lived a bit farther from her beloved mountains. One day she was exploring and found a little hideaway in some bushes. *This would make a wonderful play area for Petie.* But although her ideas blossomed into a workshop area, with a bench and tools for his play, she did not have the skills to develop it.

The old lady paused in her writing. In Barbie's tricky imagination the playhouse for her precious brother had been completed. Now the old lady remembered back to the little three year old boy with the blonde hair, blue eyes and that impish grin, and like Barbie she imagined him pounding with a little toy hammer in the hideaway his big sister had created in her mind.

Harry limped around in his new surroundings. His intelligent, active mind could see possibilities, especially in that old two-car garage that sat idle on his property. He contacted an oil company called the North Star. "Would you please put in a gas tank and fill it up with gas? I'd like to go into business. I'll pay you back as soon as I sell the gas."

Soon Harry's business opened. He loved to figure out mechanical problems and soon became the expert corner-gas business owner.

Although luxuries like nylon stockings had come on the market, Verta never had extra money to buy them. One day a travelling salesman came to their house. He looked old but seemed friendly so Verta talked to him while Barbie, now a tall, thin, nine-year-old child stood watching. The salesman explained that he was selling the new and amazing nylon stockings. "I'd like to try a pair on your daughter, so you can see for yourself how great they are." With that he pulled out a stocking and started to pull it onto Barbie's leg.

Verta watched as Barbie's face turned from excitement to bewilderment as the man pulled a stocking further and further up her leg. Then he started to explore Barbie's private area. Verta was angry. "Take your stockings and go. I never want to see you again."

Barbie stood still as if turned to stone, as she tried to understand why the old man would do such a thing. She had experienced some sexual experimentation by an older boy and his young companion once. Both of these experiences left her feeling uncomfortable and strangely guilty, of what she did not know and her mother had no words to explain.

Because the family moved in April, Barbie and Joyce had to go to a new school. So one day they set out with their mother to the Little School about four blocks away. The children sat in rows, with their desks lined up. Grades one, two, and three were all in this school, not eight like their previous school. Their teacher was Miss Hatter. She was slight and had bright red hair. As Barbie and Joyce sat in school they learned that Miss Hatter was usually very nice, but sometimes when she became angry she screamed at the children.

One morning they went to school and Miss Hatter couldn't speak. The children figured she had yelled too much the day before, although she said she had laryngitis.

Barbie was in grade three and she enjoyed class. Joyce was a grade behind. Miss Hatter asked Barbie to help some of the younger children to read. *Yes, I will be a school teacher when I grow up,* she said to herself.

The next fall Barbie went to the Middle School; it included grades four, five, and six. She really liked her new teacher, Miss Winters, who wore her hair rolled on her forehead and each side. Barbie decided that she would wear her hair just like Miss Winters.

One day Miss Winters announced a storytelling contest. Students could choose any story they wished and tell it to the class. Barbie chose the story called "The Dark Corner."

When the day came to tell the story, Barbie stood up in class and told the children of a great painter who was creating masterpieces in a large cathedral. One day someone was watching him paint one of his gorgeous paintings in a dark, hidden corner of the cathedral.

"Why are you painting such a beautiful picture where no one will see it," they asked.

"But God will see it," the painter said.

Barbie sat down and everyone clapped. When the judging was completed, she had won first prize: a clear glass salt and pepper shaker sitting on a glass tray. Prizes were almost non-existent in those days of poverty and she kept her treasured prize for a long time.

The old woman remembered how Barbie had been determined to please God in what she did, even if no one else noticed. It was as if she held that story in her mind forever.

For years Verta had longed for Christian friends, and a church to attend. In the village she met a missionary couple. They held services in a hall, school, or a home and Verta became friends with them. She reaffirmed her commitment to Jesus as Lord and Saviour at that time.

Verta soon discovered that Harry was not pleased with her decision. He had grown up in a church but had become a sceptic. Although she had given in to Harry's wishes at other times, in this she was adamant. When she told him she was going to be baptized, he locked her in the bedroom, but she waited and was baptized later without his knowledge or consent.

One day Verta said to Barbie, "Do you want to accept Jesus as Saviour too?"

"Yes," said Barbie and she made a decision that was to last her lifetime.

In retrospect the old woman could remember no time of active rebellion against God in either Verta or Barbie. Their hearts just seemed to be drawn to God and spiritual matters.

One night Harry came in and said to Verta, "It looks like war. Hitler is stirring up trouble."

Barbie listened to her Dad talk about war and feared. Would Canada be safe? Would she be safe?

But life continued and soon she put thoughts of war in the back of her mind. School was the important thing. She had to get good grades.

It was Harry's birthday and Verta sent Petie to the store with five cents to buy a chocolate bar for Harry's birthday. When Petie came home, Verta said to him, "Did you buy Daddy a chocolate bar?"

"Yes, Mommy."

"Well, where is it?"

"Uh, I just ate a little, and then I had a little more." Petie looked guilty and shuffled. Finally he showed his mother the empty chocolate bar wrapper.

One day Barbie, Joyce and Faith wandered off together and went to the river that meandered through the village.

"Let's just put our feet in the water," one of the girls said.

"Okay," said the others.

Soon they were wading up to their waist, holding up their dresses so they wouldn't get wet.

When they arrived home, they took off their wet underpants and laid them on a fence to dry.

Verta walked outside and noticed the wet clothing. "Girls, how do you get your clothes wet?"

"We waded in the river," they said.

"Joyce and Faith, I told you not to go near the river," their mother said. "I will have to spank you for disobeying. Barbie, I didn't tell you so you escape the spanking, but none of you are to go in again."

The old woman remembered that day. Verta was sad and troubled. She had never spanked the girls before; Harry was the disciplinarian, but little Jimmy's mother told her that the river had holes in it. "One child," she said, "got stuck in a hole and drowned." Verta wanted to ensure that her children were safe.

On another occasion Barbie and Joyce had misbehaved. Troubled about the possible consequences of the children's actions, Verta woke them out of their sleep and gently told them never to be naughty again. Then she kissed them and let them go back to sleep. Her gentle ways encouraged obedience. What a wonderful mother and a great model of love. (Even her one-time spanking was done because of love.)

Harry's business was booming; that is, as successful as business can be in a little village in rural Manitoba in the 1930s. They had lived in their present location for two years and he announced, "It's time to move."

The old woman smiled. The dark days were over for the little family, or were they? What lay ahead?

Chapter Five

CLIMBING

The old woman took her notepad and went outside to write. Smoke still lingered in the air from the forest fires, said to be the worst in many years. She knew rains were on their way and this hot year would soon be over. Yet, there still remained much joy in these days. A squirrel scurried across the closed gate, over the wooden fence and to the walnut tree. As he ran he scolded with a loud voice, claiming his territory.

A gentle breeze blew the leaves on the trees as a squirrel ran back with a nut in his mouth. Blackie the cat purred demanding attention while a white butterfly fluttered away.

The children's sand pile lay idle under a tree planted forty-six years ago by a precious little boy. A red toy truck and several diggers waited for the next child to play with them. So many memories the old woman had, and the pastoral scene faded as the scenes of long ago came alive.

The children ran through every room in their new home.

"This bedroom belongs to me," said Petie, as he surveyed the little room that held only a cot and a dresser. Small, though it was, it was the biggest and best he had ever had.

"And we're all going to sleep in one room," chorused Barbie, Joyce, and Faith as they jumped on the double and single bed and hoped their Dad didn't see them.

The home that Harry built was small according to modern standards but it was a palace to the family. It was new and it was theirs. The house sat on the front west part of the lot, leaving enough room on the south and east for a big garden. The soil looked black and fertile and Verta wanted to start a garden as soon as possible. In the backyard lay a pile of wood for the stoves, and the one-hole outhouse. A family newly arrived from Ukraine owned the lot to the north.

The old woman's face saddened as she thought about how people from a foreign country were treated in those days. Oh, how she longed to go back and show them love and kindness. The father spoke very little English, and people of the town laughed as they said, "Every time they have another child, he adds another cardboard box." People did not understand that out of hardship and poverty arise those with great courage and tenacity.

Besides the house, Harry built a new garage. It had a small office in the north-east corner with a counter and a cash register and some shelves that held supplies. The rest of the building was reserved for the mechanical work. In front of the building were two gas pumps and a big pole with a large North Star sign on it.

Instead of milking cows, Verta now dished up gas, vulcanized tires, and served customers. She and Harry were partners in this venture, although Harry made the major decisions and held the cash. Sometimes his wallet bulged with bills until he had an opportunity to go to the bank twenty miles away to deposit the money. If his wallet became too full, he stashed some of the money in an old, empty Brownie camera hidden in the dirt cellar of their new home. Soon the business became so successful that Harry hired help.

Barbie admired the new hired man, Dave, and her smiles grew wide when he called her "Sunshine." She was twelve and he was about twenty-five years old. She and her girlfriend, Wilma, giggled and argued about who would wash his dirty socks.

Oh, young infatuation, thought the old woman. How could the girls have been so naïve and silly? She remembered how Barbie and another girlfriend found a book of love letters, carefully copied one out, and sent it to Jack—the boy Barbie had noted as mischievous in Grade A. He never answered. The old woman laughed. Barbie's grandchildren would be shocked at her stupidity.

Barbie woke up one morning with her eyelid swollen so much that it touched the lens of her glasses. Her mother took her to the optometrist in Dauphin and he referred her to a specialist in Winnipeg, her first trip to the big city. They booked into a hotel and went to the specialist. He looked at Barbie's eye and said to Verta, "I will have to operate, but first go to the hotel and keep putting on hot wet towels over that eye and bring her back to me in two days."

When they returned the swelling had subsided and Barbie sat in the Doctor's big chair. He put a clamp on her eyelid and pulled it back in order to work on the growth. Over and over he swore at Barbie and said, "Sit still!"

Barbie sat as still as a stone on a prairie field. With the operation over, the doctor turned to Verta and said, "She sure is made of good stuff."

Barbie knew better. It was not her "good stuff." She was petrified with terror.

Dave didn't stay long working at the garage. He was followed by a sixteen-year-old named Brian. Now there was only four years' difference between him and Barbie. He was her first boyfriend.

Barbie liked to watch Brian. He was thin and athletic. In his off-hours he came into the house and sat on the chair backwards—hopping over it as though it were part of an obstacle course. One day he shinnied up the North Star pole in front of the garage as supple as a monkey.

Even more daring, Brian climbed the derrick on which Harry had placed a wind charger at the back of the garage; jumping from crossbars to crossbars in leaps and bounds.

Barbie watched in great admiration at his agility and bravery.

Though Barbie's lameness had disappeared, she suffered with back problems that often kept her in bed. Her parents had no knowledge that instead of rest, activity should be prescribed. In fact, they restricted her activities in the belief that they were helping her improve. Joyce and Faith had to bring pails of water from the neighbours and carry in the wood. "You do the dishes," they said to Barbie. "That won't hurt your back."

The summer before Barbie turned thirteen Harry and Verta took her to Winnipeg to visit a famed chiropractor. He adjusted Barbie's back and told her parents that he would like to do a series of adjustments on it. They talked to a woman friend whom Verta loved and respected, and who lived in Winnipeg. Her name was Mrs. McKay. "Would you be willing to let Barbie stay with you while she travels back and forth to the chiropractor's for treatments?"

After conferring with her husband, she said, "Yes."

And that started an adventure for this twelve-year-old girl from rural Manitoba who went to live in the big city, more than two hundred miles away from Mom and Dad. Barbie had never been afraid to try something new.

Mrs. McKay was a kind woman who spoke with a Scottish accent. She showed Barbie her room and told her that she could have a bath in the white enamel tub. Barbie was awed by all the modern conveniences. There was even a flush toilet. She didn't have to go to an outhouse.

Barbie's main task was to find her way across to the other side of Winnipeg on the city busses to see the chiropractor. After being instructed on how to use the transit system, Barbie set out alone. She quickly learned her transfer points, and the landmarks that indicated her exits.

One day she had her head turned and failed to see her exit cue. She thought, "I'll just go to the end of the line and on the way back I'll see it and get off." Because she had lots of time the chiropractor and her caregivers never found out. Only the bus driver knew.

On the first Sunday morning, Mr. & Mrs. McKay invited her to go with them to a church in another part of town. Barbie had never been to a big city church and she loved it. Later in the afternoon she asked Mrs. McKay if she might go to church that evening.

"We're not going tonight," Mrs. McKay said, "but you can go by yourself if you want. When you return, ask for a transfer and get off the streetcar at Eaton's Store on Portage Avenue and wait for a bus across the street."

So that evening Barbie went to church in the big city all by herself; however, problems arose on her way home. As she rode the streetcar, she searched the darkened street to try to see Eaton's Store, but she couldn't read any of the signs. A man who sat near her said, "Are you having trouble? Are you trying to find Portage and Main?"

Not wanting to appear stupid, Barbie said, "Yes."

"Well, this is your stop," he said. "You better get off."

Her Dad had taught her to obey her elders so Barbie did as she was told. She walked up and down the street looking for Eaton's Store. "What does a person do," she thought, "when you are lost?"

"Find a policeman," Barbie said to herself. As she looked up and down trying to locate a policeman among all the walkers, she noticed that she was standing beside Eaton's Store. Still clutching her transfer ticket, she climbed on the next bus and kept her problems secret in case Mrs. McKay wouldn't let her go to church by herself again.

The old woman shuddered as she thought of the freedom Barbie was given at such a young age. Yet, Barbie had no fear. She wondered if God sent his guardian angel to look after a naïve little girl who thought she was old enough and wise enough to do anything and go anywhere.

Mrs. McKay thought that Barbie should have a friend, so she introduced her to a girl about the same age, Shirley Brown. Chatting away, Barbie went with her to an apartment. There she met Shirley's mother who looked thin, weak and ill. Barbie learned that Mrs. Brown recently had tuberculosis.

One day Shirley and Barbie were in McKay's two-storey house alone. Barbie was getting ready to go to the chiropractor and Shirley was in the washroom watching her comb her hair.

Suddenly, they heard a sound like footsteps. Barbie thought it might be her hostess' brother so said, "Hughie, is that you?" Barbie continued to call out as the soft noises continued, but there was no answer.

The girls tiptoed down the stairs afraid that it might be a burglar. A sudden noise startled them and they dashed for the nearby front door. They walked down the sidewalk toward the street and noticed a man walking by. Should they ask for help? But he was a stranger and they were in the city, so they decided against it. They walked back to the front door planning to open it and look inside. To their chagrin, the door had automatically locked. They peeked in the window and noticed the door to the silverware cabinet ajar. Terror gripped them but they had nowhere to go for help.

They walked over to Shirley's apartment. Because Shirley's mother was ill the girls didn't want to burden her with their worries, so with an uneasy mind Barbie borrowed transit money and took Shirley along to her appointment.

Shirley had been invited for dinner, and when the she and Barbie returned late in the afternoon, Mr. & Mrs. McKay and guests were just starting to eat. The girls joined them. During the meal Barbie said to Mrs. McKay, "Was everything all right when you came home? Your silverware was okay, was it?"

Mrs. McKay looked at her, "Tell me, what is all this about? Why are you asking those questions?" And Barbie's story came tumbling out. Mrs. McKay smiled as the corners of her eyes wrinkled and she said, "You heard the wind flapping the Venetian blinds. The windows were open. I often hear that noise."

Soon Barbie's time in the big city concluded and Barbie was put on the train. Her Dad had driven her to Winnipeg and she had never ridden the train before. She was familiar with it because several times a day it arrived in their village to get water for the steam that propelled the train's engines. It then loaded up with freight, mail, and passengers. It had taken almost three hours for her Dad to make the trip and she thought she might need a snack before she arrived home, so she bought a bag of oranges.

Barbie climbed on the train when the conductor called, "All aboard!" After he took her ticket, Barbie settled down to watch the scenery. She used the washroom with the wooden seat and the open hole that showed the rail tracks underneath. A sign said, "Do not use the toilet when the train is stopped."

It seemed to Barbie that the train stopped at every little clearing. She noticed other people going to the dining room where the chef, resplendent in his white jacket and cap, served them. But Barbie had very little money and she opened her bag of oranges. The day dragged on…and on…and on, and she continued to eat oranges. When she left the train she felt nauseated and just got home in time to vomit in the biffy—she had eaten too many oranges!

Barbie was a quiet girl. Her world was composed of home, school, and the Bible studies that the missionaries held. Between her studies and the responsibilities of being the eldest child, she had little extra time. Nevertheless, whenever possible she and her friend Wilma took walks around the neighbourhood and talked kid-stuff, although to them it was grown-up information.

"I'm really upset," said Barbie, "Petie was playing at the Fuhrs. He and his friend Ernest climbed on a shed roof and Ernest pushed him off and Petie hurt his head."

"I wouldn't put up with that," said Wilma. "You should tell Mrs. Fuhr off. She should teach her son better."

The two girls continued walking and talking about the accident until they saw Mrs. Fuhr working in her garden.

By this time, Barbie's indignation had peaked and she proceeded to scold her mother's friend.

Quietly, Mrs. Fuhr replied, "I'm sorry, Barbie, that Petie got hurt. I'll try to watch them better next time."

As the girls walked away, Wilma said, "I know I told you to tell her off but I didn't really think you would do it."

For over seventy years, the old woman felt grieved at Barbie's actions. Mrs. Fuhr was such a kind woman: a turn-the-other-cheek person and Barbie had acted like a brat. The old woman thought it gracious that Mrs. Fuhr never told Barbie's mother. Mrs. Fuhr's love and humility was a notable part of her personality.

One day as Barbie and Wilma were walking, Wilma said, "My mother is never going to speak to your mother again. She is mad at her." Being such grown-up young women, they discussed the matter.

"Well, I side with my mother," said Barbie.

"And I side with my mother," said Wilma.

At that they agreed that they would not be best friends and they rarely spoke to each other.

Strange, thought the old woman. It was a good friendship and Barbie loved her best friend. Yet, as children they knew where their loyalties lay.

Up to this time Barbie had not seen an airplane. One day as the children sat in the classroom they heard a strange sound. It was an airplane. Teacher allowed them to race to the windows and see it!

Soon after that day the students heard a knock at the classroom door. After the teacher answered it, he turned to Barbie and said, "Your Dad has come for you. You may go with him."

Outside the schoolhouse, Barbie saw Joyce, Faith, and Petie all sitting in a strange car. "This is now our new car," said her Dad. "Get in. I'll take you all for a ride." Wow, a grand new car—a 1940 Hudson. It was a beauty, and the children loved it.

As Daddy drove out in the isolated countryside, he let each of the younger children in turn sit on his knee and hold the wheel while he maintained control.

Barbie was too old to sit on his knee. So one day, he let her drive as he sat in the passenger's seat. Once more they went out in the country where there was seldom any traffic. All went well, as Barbie concentrated on the task. Suddenly, the car started to go down a hill and it kept going faster and faster. Barbie panicked. Quietly, her Dad said, "Ease up a bit on the gas."

Harry's wind charger was hooked to a generator and motor that ran all day until late evening, generating electricity for his garage and home. Sometimes when Barbie awoke at one or two a.m. she still could hear the motor going and knew her Dad was still working. He had the first electricity in the area. In each room there was a light hanging from a wire. From it dangled a string to change the light from off to on, etc. Harry's constant reminder to the children was, "When you leave the room, turn off the light."

Harry's demands dominated the family, thought the old woman. "Where's dinner?" "Where are my keys; everyone look." "Turn off those lights." "Don't." "No!"

Yet, the old woman understood Harry. It was through much work and sacrifice that he provided for his family. Harry seldom stopped working, although he slept in Sunday morning and occasionally watched a movie or played cards with friends. Other than that, he worked tirelessly. She had seen him pass out from exhaustion and lack of food.

One day the children invited a friend named Curly into the house to play with them. They thought their Dad would not approve but he was at work. Suddenly, they saw him coming home. "Hide," they said to Curly and shoved him behind a tall black chest of drawers where he hid until their father left. The children were saved from their father's wrath; and Curly never returned to play with them.

Harry and Verta were away for the evening. "*Let's have some fun,*" said the girls. They pulled out one of their mother's recipe books and looked for a candy recipe. "Ah, toffee; let's make this."

They carefully measured the ingredients, one of which was a cup of molasses. When the toffee was cooked they tried it. It didn't taste very good. There was too much molasses in the recipe. "Let's put some puffed wheat in it," said Barbie. Now they had oodles of toffee to eat and it still tasted like molasses. Finally they hid it in the cupboard where their Dad would not see it. Later their Mom found it and quietly threw it out.

Yet, for all of his harshness Harry had tender moments. One day he was invited to sing at the funeral of a friend. Pale and tense he began, *Rock of Ages, cleft for...* then fell to the floor and lost consciousness. He never talked of his embarrassment, nor did he ever sing in public again. The world lost the sound of a beautiful tenor voice.

The previous year, Harry had come into the house and announced that World War Two had started. During the First World War, though only fourteen years old, he had run away from home and enlisted in the army.

Letters from England had been important events in Harry's life. They were his only contact with his birth family and the mother he adored. His father had died when Harry was twenty-six years old. After the war started, Harry's mother wrote that she was going to live in a big house in Wales, far from the site of most bombings.

One day the family received a letter from Harry's mother. It was the family habit for anyone in the family to read letters from England. Barbie picked up her Granny's letter and started to read:

"Don't you think that Barbie is a most original girl? Her letters are really clever. Please do not tell her I said so, or they will be spoilt. Perhaps she hears too much grown-up talk, and too much gossip—but they are splendid letters, and I appreciate them."

Barbie blushed and put the letter down; her feelings were hurt. Did her grandmother not know that she was grown-up; and what she had written was just information, not gossip?

To this day, thought the old woman, Barbie treasured that single page of the last letter Granny wrote to the family.

Still the old woman knew that Barbie's grandmother's perceptions were accurate. Her granddaughter did spend too much time with adults, participating in adult conversations, and following adult pursuits.

Barbie achieved full height by age twelve and thereafter believed herself to be an adult with responsibilities. Sometimes it was given to her and sometimes she assumed it in the absence of her parents. Barbie tried to rise to the many challenges.

During early teens Barbie had assisted with both Sunday School classes and children's Vacation Bible School. Now the missionary's wife became pregnant and gave up her job of storytelling. It fell to Barbie. The weekly ritual was to choose, learn, and tell the story to three different audiences in three different locations: in a house in Ochre River, a little mountain church, or one of the many country school houses that dotted neighbouring areas.

Yes, acknowledged the old woman, Barbie certainly had many adult responsibilities. Somehow she didn't think Barbie had been damaged by them though.

Harry walked in the house. His face was white with anger. An enemy warplane on its way to London had problems and the pilot needed to turn back to Germany.

Before he did, he dropped his bomb on a lone house in Wales. The house even had large balloons over it to discourage bombers, but somehow the enemy plane got through. The home was destroyed and all within it, including Harry's mother.

"That's it," said Harry. "I am joining the Air Force."

Once his mind was made up, Harry never dallied over a decision. He enlisted in the Royal Canadian Air Force and was sent to a training camp in Ontario.

Barbie was excited. Her Dad was coming home. When he stepped off the train she noticed that he looked handsome in his Air Force uniform. The best part was that he brought presents for everyone. Her mother looked beautiful in her new white dress with red buttons and matching wide-brimmed white hat with red trim. Faith resembled a cherished princess in her pink taffeta with wine-coloured decorations. Barbie and Joyce each received a blue crepe dress with a smocked yoke, and Petie, a blue suit. Harry had an eye for style and his taste was impeccable.

Soon Harry returned to training camp, leaving Verta to run the garage with the help of a hired man. In addition to all the other duties, she added running a taxi service with the Hudson car. Monthly payments had to be made on it.

Sometimes the children would come home from school and their Mom was not to be found. Barbie felt the cold and emptiness of the house without her but soon looked in the cupboards to find some bread, or potatoes to fry, so the other children and she could eat.

To make meals more interesting, Barbie decided to start baking for the family. One day at a neighbour's Barbie ate a piece of cake. "Your cake is really good," she said. "Would you please give me your recipe?"

Recipe in hand, Barbie stoked up the wood-burning cook stove, took out the ingredients and began to make the cake. As it baked, she noticed a strange smell emanating from the oven. She peeked in to see how the cake was doing. It didn't resemble the rich chocolate of her neighbour's.

When the cake was done, they discovered the problems. Someone had put liniment in the vanilla bottle, and the neighbour had omitted the cocoa from the recipe. Soon after, some friends came to visit as Barbie was scraping out the cake intending to throw it down the outside toilet. One of the neighbours, Mrs. French, said, "What a waste! Don't you know it's wartime and sugar is rationed? If you don't want to eat it, put it out for the neighbourhood dogs and cats."

The old woman smiled. Barbie always tried to please, but she noticed that some neighbourhood pets became ill soon after Barbie put the cake out.

Ration cards were given to families and they were only allowed a limited amount of sugar and gas. Every time they were used, the cards were punched, and once the allotment was gone none could be purchased until the next month.

By 1941 Harry had been honourably discharged from the Air Force because of ill health. The rationing proved an annoyance to Harry. There was nothing he could do about gas rationing, but he enjoyed his sweets. To counteract the loss of sugar, he decided to keep bees.

Some weeks later Harry put on coveralls and a hood with facial screening to keep the bees away, and went out to gather the honey. Barbie stood with the other children at the kitchen window watching. As he began, they noticed Harry slap one leg and then the other. Before long he repeatedly jumped up and down. He had not tied up his pant legs and the bees crawled up his legs and thighs and continued to sting him multiple times. Barbie noticed that despite his love for sugar, the bee hives were soon removed.

Late one night, Harry had an emergency taxi call. A young pregnant First Natives woman was having difficulties. She asked him to take her to the nearest hospital twenty miles away. Before reaching the hospital, the woman gave birth as Harry assisted. The grateful mother named the baby "Harry" after her taxi driver, and Harry had to tolerate the good-natured ribbing of all his friends and customers.

On rare occasions Verta put up a quilting frame in their living room, and women of the neighbourhood joined her in a quilting bee. Other times one of her best friends, Mrs. Marshall, joined her, and together they brewed a pot of paste on the stove, measured and cut strips of wallpaper, and after brushing paste on the back, smoothed the strips on the wall. They finished the room with a decorative border at the top.

Verta liked creating. Her talents came alive when making something for the house, sewing a dress for a child, growing a beautiful garden, or creating a gift for one of the girls to take to a birthday party.

Besides her creative talents, the local doctor, 'Doc', frequently called on her to help him with operations or to deliver a baby. Although she had no medical training, she followed instructions well, and stayed calm during emergencies. There was no hospital for many miles and no other available medical help if doc was out of town. So mothers in labour often called Verta, and she became adept at delivering babies. Whatever situation occurred, she always had a 'can-do' attitude!

Once Verta was called as a witness in a court case. During that time Verta's garter broke. It held up her stocking and she wasn't free to leave and fix the problem. She used a life-saver candy as a substitute!

One day a man requested a taxi ride to the northern town of Le Pas, Manitoba. Harry insisted that this was Verta's job as he was busy in the garage. It would be a long, hard trip over primitive roads; some of them were still corduroy (logs laid crossways to form a road).

At home Barbie (now fourteen years old) made the meals while Joyce did the housecleaning. The day before her mother was to return, Barbie decided to surprise her mother and wash all the dirty clothes. She pulled the old wringer washer and rinse tub to the middle of the kitchen, filled them with warm water heated on the wood stove, and began the task. After each load was finished, she carried the clothes outside and fastened them to the wire line with wooden clothespins. The line stretched between two poles the length of the backyard. When Barbie finished hanging up the clothes, she drained the washing machine, carried the dirty water outside and dumped it. Then she emptied the rinse tub and tidied up the work area.

It had been a big task but Barbie had done it; the first time she had washed clothes all by herself. She heaved a big sigh and grabbed the novel that she was reading. Soon the book captivated her and she lost touch with reality.

Barbie always seemed to be reading some book. Maybe, it would have been better if she had more friends and lived fully in the real world. Late on school nights Verta would often say to Barbie, "Time to turn off the light and go to sleep." Barbie consistently said, "Aw, Mom, can't I read another chapter?"

After a while Barbie became conscious that wind and rain pounded the little house. "I wonder how the clothes are doing?" she said to herself. She looked out the back door. The clothes line had broken, and wet clothes lay on the mud-soaked dirt of the garden. Barbie put on some boots and a coat and picked up the clothes, and piled them into the rinse tub and washing machine. The lovely surprise she had planned for her mother turned out to be a disaster.

The next day Verta arrived home weary from the long trip. She looked at the piles of wet, dirty clothes and started to work.

The old woman wondered where Verta's patience came from. She might have been very angry with Barbie, but wasn't. Instead she looked at the intent, not the outcome of the act.

Once a friend said to Barbie, "If you are half the woman your mother is when you grow up, you will be a great woman." The old woman never heard Barbie talk about it, but she knew that Barbie never forgot.

Harry and Verta had arranged for Barbie to travel to Winnipeg for another session at the chiropractor's. This time when she arrived at their friend's home, Mrs. McKay said, "Barbie, I am going away and have arranged for you to stay at the Big Sisters. It's an organization for girls and they have a home where you can live while going to your appointments."

The women who ran Big Sisters welcomed Barbie. She was shown to her bed in a big room with several beds occupied by other girls. All of the girls looked different. There were blondes, brunettes, and red heads, and their personalities were as diverse as the colours of their hair. A sign hung on the wall. Barbie read, "Before getting into bed all girls must have a bath."

So every night, obedient to the sign, Barbie bathed in the big tub. Except one night she didn't feel like having a bath. She walked down the backstairs to the kitchen. "Is it okay if I don't have a bath tonight? I'm tired," said Barbie.

One of the ladies laughed. "You mean you thought that sign meant '*every night.*' You were just supposed to bath the first night before you got into bed. We wondered who was using all the hot water."

Barbie's face turned pink. She mumbled "Thank you" and walked back upstairs.

Back home once more, Barbie noticed that her Dad was getting restless. The war still dragged on and Harry wanted to take part in the war effort. Some friends told him of a plant in Montreal that had been converted into manufacturing machine parts for defence. One day he announced his decision to the family: "Pack your bags; we're all moving to Montreal."

Yes, thought the old woman, Harry was capable and intelligent, but always restless. The business had grown much in the past two years and now he was ready for a new challenge. So he boarded up the garage and walked away from it.

Chapter Six

MOVING AGAIN

The old woman finished her breakfast, put a load in the automatic washer, and walked outdoors. The cows grazed in the fields enclosed with barbwire fencing. One young calf gazed at her with inquisitive eyes and continued to munch. She looked at the morning skies scattered with misty, high clouds while the sun sent its advance party of rays that shone in the eastern sky. This morning she must resume Barbie's story. So many years had passed; so many memories.

The family stood outside their garage waiting for a bus that would take them to a connecting train in Winnipeg. Muriel, Verta's sister-in-law, also travelled with her children to Montreal. The men were driving because Harry wanted to have his car in the big city.

One child stood tall in the midst of the children. It was Barbie. Faith held her treasured dolly in her arms, and

Joyce stood politely waiting, while Petie danced around with mischief in his cute blue eyes.

Barbie had been feeling ill, so the doctor prescribed sleeping pills for the trip. When the train stopped in Sudbury, they briefly got off to say hello to Aunt Emily who was stationed nearby. When Barbie saw her she said, "Emily, you've dyed your hair red!"

Emily laughed, even though it was an era when only bold and daring women would dye their hair. Seven years older than Barbie, they had always had friendly relations. Earlier Barbie had bet her a quarter that she would be married before she was eighteen years old. A few months before Emily's birthday, she came to see Barbie and paid her the quarter. Now a married woman of twenty-one, she and her husband were both in the military.

The family waved goodbye to Emily and climbed back on the train as the conductor yelled, "All aboard!" The train wound around the northern part of Ontario. Barbie gazed at the miles and miles of swamp and fir trees with very little signs of human life. She still felt ill and continued taking the sleeping pills. Barbie roused from her induced stupor to see the capital city, Ottawa. Soon they were alighting in Montreal where their father met them. Driving, the men had arrived in the city ahead of the women and children.

Ah, the big wonderful Montreal where almost everyone seemed to speak a foreign language, and where Barbie couldn't understand one word. Her Dad drove them to their rented apartment in Verdun. They had a second-storey apartment in a new row of apartments in an area still under development, a short distance from the St. Lawrence River. Aunt Muriel and Uncle Ernie and children rented the apartment below them.

Barbie's father had furnished their apartment simply and adequately, but before the family arrived, Uncle Ernie had all his money stolen from the hotel room when he was away working. Now his family slept on blankets on the floor until he could earn more money. Uncle Ernie had managed to buy food with his first cheque. They sat around a big cardboard box to eat. A neighbour peeked in their home and spread the word about their living conditions. In order to quell the gossip, word went out that their furniture was still to arrive from Manitoba.

Barbie said goodbye to the other children as they set off for their first day in the big English-speaking school. A bit frightened and still somewhat ill from the sleeping pills and the trip, she was glad to hear her parents say she didn't have to go to school. In fact, because of their leniency and the lack of emphasis on a proper education, Barbie stayed out of school for that whole year. She found her niche in the youth group of an English-speaking church and fell in love with the big city.

Verta had always been and continued to be a 'lady.' She held herself with grace and looked elegant in her clothes. In addition, she had a charm that came from a spirit of love, consideration, and respect for others.

One day when she needed their only family car, she decided to drive Harry across Montreal to his work site and then use the car for her errands. It was early morning, and she quickly put on the satin housecoat that matched the blue of her eyes.

"I'll be okay dressed like this," she said to Harry. "I won't even have to get out of the car."

She dropped Harry off at the entrance to his work and started on her return trip. While still in downtown Montreal the car stopped. Here she was in the busy metropolis, in her gorgeous gown, with a disabled car, and a mechanic who spoke only French. Somehow, she managed to convey her need, get the car fixed, and return home slightly embarrassed.

Montreal during this era hustled and bustled with people of all descriptions, among them men and women of the army, navy, and air force as well as extra defence workers and the usual citizens of a big city.

Gas was still rationed, and comic books and cartoons depicted people hanging out the windows and the open front and rear doors of street cars as they travelled from stop to stop.

One day Verta and Barbie ventured downtown to shop. When they finished, they waited in line as the streetcar lumbered up to them in comic book fashion. People crowded in. Verta got her feet on the step of the streetcar expecting Barbie to follow, but there was no more room and the street car started off.

Barbie stood there stunned. Her mother was gone and she was alone with strangers milling around her. "Oh, well, I guess I will just have to get on the next one." Barbie waited at the front of the line and got on the next car. When the car arrived at the next stop, her mother stood at the head of the line. Verta had exited the streetcar at the first stop, and much relieved she joined her daughter.

Verta liked to provide for her children even on a limited income. Once she showed Barbie a coat she had bought second-hand. "This coat is so warm," she said to Barbie. "It will protect you in the coldest weather."

Barbie looked at it and tried to show enthusiasm. Her mother was so kind but Barbie hated the coat. She tried it on and thought it made her look like a fat, furry animal, but to please her Mom she wore it—for awhile. Gradually it became clear to Verta that her wonderful purchase was not appreciated and true to her nature she never forced Barbie to wear it.

One day Verta saw an ad in the paper. There was a coat and matching hat that would just fit Joyce. When she picked up the coat, Joyce was ecstatic. It was perfect.

A couple of days later, Joyce said, "Mom, I'm going to wash my hair. It's itchy."

It wasn't long before Joyce said to her mother, "I've washed my hair, Mom, and the itch isn't any better. It's driving me crazy."

Verta went to Joyce, parted her hair and looked. "Joyce, you're lousy." Joyce began to cry. The second-hand coat and hat had carried some little passengers. Verta went to the drug store and bought some treatment. Not only Joyce, but all the children were deloused.

Life in Montreal soon became routine. Harry went to work everyday. The family enjoyed their relatives who lived downstairs and they were beginning to make friends. One day a curious neighbour began to quiz Verta about the length of time she and Harry were married. Innocently, little Faith had given inaccurate information about her parents' marriage, and the ages of the children. The dates didn't add up. Despite the neighbour's lack of finesse, Verta laughed it off and told the truth. She had nothing to hide.

The one constant in Verta and the children's lives was the church they attended. Barbie and Joyce took a bus and went during the week to take lessons in French from the Pastor. One of their first tasks was to memorize and recite a Bible verse in French. It was John 3:16: *For God so loved the world that he gave his only begotten Son, that whosoever believeth in him should not perish, but have eternal life.*(King James Version)

In addition to the French studies, Barbie enrolled in an adult correspondence course in Theology through Winnipeg Bible School. She enjoyed the studies and whether by their kindness or not she managed to get good grades.

Barbie was intensely loyal to her mother. One night Verta prepared the evening meal. Harry did not come home, nor did he call. Hours later he and Uncle Ernie walked in, and he demanded supper. Harry gave no explanation for their tardiness. Barbie served her Dad and uncle the warmed-up food. As she served, anger flashed in her eyes. Later, Uncle Ernie said to her with a twinkle in his eyes, "I thought you were going to hit your Dad over the head with that cast iron frying pan."

The old woman laid down her pen. Barbie had not learned yet that love covers a multitude of sins. Though a Christian, she had no idea of the power and value of unconditional love and forgiveness. Oh, well, the old woman thought, I can't change Barbie, the teenager of many years ago.

The family lived in Montreal for about a year. During that time World War Two continued unabated. Enemy U-Boats were seen entering the St. Lawrence River. The city decided to prepare in case of an enemy attack and scheduled an Air Raid Drill. During the drill, homeowners were told to shut off all lights and pull curtains. When the siren sounded, Verta and the children hurried around and followed instructions. A second siren blew and, assuming that meant the end of the air raid drill, they turned on all the lights again. Men pounded at their door. "Turn off your lights! It's an air raid drill!" It was then the family learned that the first siren was only a warning. The second alarm signalled the actual air raid drill.

To Barbie the interesting thing about the whole experience was peeking out the windows and seeing the lights of Mount Royal going off one by one, and after the drill watching the lights gradually coming alive.

One day, Harry came home from work with an angry and determined look on his face. He had been promoted to foreman soon after he took the job, but now he had an argument with someone in authority. In anger he quit his job. "We're moving back to Manitoba," he said.

Barbie looked at him and said, "Dad, can I stay here? I love Montreal."

"No!" he said. "Start packing."

Soon they were back in Ochre River. The garage that had been boarded up was reopened and family life resumed.

Ten-year-old Faith looked around the village. "How come the stores and houses are all smaller," she said, "and they all need to be painted?" The village hadn't changed but Faith's perceptions had.

Little Petie had just turned eight years old and was happy to get back to play with his many friends.

Joyce, in her quiet gracious manner, gently took up life where she had left off, while Barbie had a big decision to make.

In the village there was a small telephone office in which a young woman sat, managing a switch board. She was called the Operator or Central. Her job was to connect the caller with the desired party. The Operator resigned her job and Barbie, now almost fifteen years of age, looked very mature and capable. Someone suggested she apply for the job.

Barbie asked her Mom and Dad what she should do. Her choices were to go back to school or apply for the job. Both her mother and father gave her the same answer, "It is your decision. We're not deciding for you."

Barbie's decision was difficult. On one hand the job would give her money and independence; on the other hand, she had some vague idea that more education would be an excellent idea. She decided to go back to school. It had been her own decision and she decided to put her heart and energies into getting excellent grades. Although her grade eight class was small and achievement insignificant, she vied for top grades with another girl.

There were three schools in the village. The first one was called the Little School and now held a combined class of grade one and two students. Middle School consisted of one class of grades three, four, and five. High School had two classes. The downstairs class held students in grades six, seven, and eight, and the upstairs class consisted of the rest of the High School students. High School studies in Manitoba at that time finished in grade eleven but had high academic standards.

Students were expected to work hard and enjoyed no frills like field trips, or extra school sports teams. School hours were nine a.m. to four p.m. with a one-hour break for lunch and two recesses of fifteen minutes each. During the recesses it was expected that every student would play softball. Barbie hated softball with a passion. Although her lameness had disappeared, she was not athletic. She couldn't see the ball properly and couldn't judge distances; with these disabilities she was always chosen last.

Physical Education was in the form of drill. Once Barbie played soccer and she liked that, as the ball was big enough for her to see and she was athletic enough to kick it and sometimes even score a goal. But soccer never became the school's game of choice and she was stuck with softball. Barbie coaxed to become scorekeeper. Sometimes the teachers granted her that privilege.

Social Studies involved study of World War Two that was still raging. Although war had not reached Canada, fear was rife that the Nazi regime under Hitler and the Japanese could together conquer the world. Teachers tracked the occupation of Europe on the map as Hitler continued to conquer countries across Europe. Barbie looked at the enemy-occupied country and feared for Canada, their family, and relatives. Their village was full of airmen resplendent in their blue uniforms, as there were two airports nearby. Barbie and Joyce walked the streets enjoying the admiring glances of the military men, while Petie and his friends searched for downed drogue parachutes that could be picked up and sold.

Planes from the airports trailed a drogue-parachute so that airmen in another plane could practice shooting at it as it followed about 100 feet behind the plane. Sometimes, the drogue was cut free by the shot and fell to the earth. The Royal Canadian Air Force valued these and paid children a small sum for retrieving them—more if the cable was still attached. It seemed like a small fortune to children in those days.

It was in High School that the teacher decided the students would put on a three act play, named "The Prodigal Son." Barbie was chosen to play one of the major roles, the choir leader.

The night of the play Barbie peeked out at the audience, many of whom were crying at the drama. The play proved to be an amazing success. They were invited to perform it in a neighbouring village the next week.

A missionary who held unusually strict beliefs talked to Barbie, "You have done wrong by acting in the play. You must stop."

"Stop," thought Barbie, "but why, and how? I have done nothing wrong." She knew the play had a good moral and, besides, by refusing to act she would betray the whole school. She had to perform. So she did, even though after the concert, she was violently sick to her stomach. She had been given an impossible order. Once more she acted independently and according to her conscience.

One day when Barbie was visiting friends, her host came up behind her and cupped both her breasts with his hands. Barbie's main training on sexuality had come from a medical book that her mother left where the children could find it. His breathing was fast and Barbie realized he was out of control. His wife was in the next room and Barbie did not want to alert her. "No. No. Don't," she whispered, and wriggled out of his grasp but his behaviour haunted her for years.

His wife never realized what had happened and Barbie never told her mother or anyone else. She didn't want to tarnish his reputation; besides, she feared her father's rage if he heard about it.

Barbie had seen his protective anger once before. She was in the garage office when an inebriated customer came in and tried to force her to take a drink from his bottle.

Her father entered and said, "Stop immediately! She is underage. When she is of age and drinks, that is to be her choice. No one is going to force her."

The man left and Barbie sighed. For once she appreciated her Dad's anger.

Barbie's first boy friend, Brian, had joined the Air Force and was stationed in Newfoundland. She imagined she was in love. Barbie enjoyed the letters from him and liked the pair of salt and pepper shakers made from silver bullets that he had sent her.

The old woman laid down her pen as memories of wartime threatened to overwhelm her. Even children experienced fear and hatred for the enemy instead of empathy for the thousands and thousands injured and dying. The survival instinct seemed to take precedence and stifle compassion, except for those in one's inner circle. The old woman remembered how Barbie and all her friends longed to be old enough to join the fight. They had no idea how fortunate they were to be exempt.

One day Barbie received a letter from Brian saying that he loved her. Barbie was giddy with joy as she anticipated his coming letters. Week after week she waited, but his letters never came. Then one day she went to see his mother in the next town. "Have you heard from Brian lately?" she said.

"Hasn't he written you?" His mother's voice was anxious. "I'll tell him to send you a letter."

Barbie was puzzled. *Had his last letter not said that he loved her? What could be wrong?*

About two weeks later she opened his pale blue airmail letter from Newfoundland (not yet a province of Canada). She read the words, "I am married."

Wow, what bomb hit Barbie? Later her grandmother said to her, "Do you know what I said when I heard what Brian did?"

"No," Barbie said, "probably 'Good.'"

With that the subject was dropped. Her practical grandmother moved on to another subject and Barbie was left to wonder, *but why?*

That was the best thing that ever happened to Barbie, muttered the old woman. Barbie didn't seem to mourn very much over lost love. She doubted whether Barbie even knew what love really was.

Another year passed and Barbie was now in the upstairs class. The little lab room held a big bell that the teacher rang to signal the beginning or end of classes. If it happened to be the end of class, he would come back into the room and dismiss the students. Sometimes he rang the bell to signal fire drill. The upstairs classroom had an escape ramp that could be accessed through an open window. Through it students could slide down; however, this route was never used during Barbie's school days. When the fire drill bell sounded, the students were free to walk out the door, down the stairs and outside to safety without first being dismissed.

One day the teacher left the room and the word was whispered around, "Fire Drill!" So the students were ready and waiting, and on the first peal of the bell they all rushed to and out the door and down the stairs. As he left the lab, he met the students exiting his classroom. He stood with his mouth wide open, amazed at the audacity of his students. It was recess and he had not dismissed the class.

In those days, students were rigidly controlled by the teacher. Barbie had escaped as far as grade nine with never a reprimand. One day she whispered something to her cousin who sat in the seat in front of her desk. The teacher scolded her. Her face reddened. She felt that she was now a young woman and beyond criticism.

In grade nine Barbie finally learned how to get a good mark in art. Art (as in most subjects) was strictly taught. In the early grades the teacher would put an object in front of the student and say, "Draw it." Though most of the time Barbie excelled she was not a top art student and felt that she was a failure. However, in grade nine, she learned that the teacher usually asked for a drawing of a scene. So Barbie took an art book and studied the composition of a scene drawn by a famous artist. And every time she had an exam, she drew the scene but adjusted it to the various seasons of the year and altered other details. Thereafter, she always got acceptable grades in her weak subject.

One of the joys of High School was running home for lunch to their house just a block and one half away. When she burst into the kitchen she quickly turned on the radio to hear a loud double knock.

"Who's there?"

"It's the Happy Gang," called out Bert Pearl in his jolly, enthusiastic manner. Then the music and singing began, "Keep happy. It's the Happy Gang." Later on in the program if Barbie was lucky, Eddie Allen would sing, "And someday by the River of the Roses, we'll meet again." Although Barbie never met Bert Pearl and Eddie Allen, they were her teenage idols.

Barbie's friend, Lena, invited her to her home in the country, where she met Lena's uncle, Gordon, who had polio as a baby. While the rest of his body grew normally, his legs did not develop properly and could not hold his body up.

Barbie admired Gordon's courage, determination, and cheerfulness. He had no wheelchair and moved by dragging and pulling himself. It was winter during her visit, and she watched as Gordon went outside and hitched a big dog to a sleigh and went for a ride. Although Barbie seldom saw Gordon, he made a profound effect on her, and influenced her life's direction.

One day Harry came into the house. Barbie and her mother were standing in the living room. Harry said to Verta, "I am leaving you and taking the car."

Immediately Barbie's anger burst the bounds she had placed on it. She had seen her gentle mother disrespected and mentally overpowered by this man who was her father. She knew that her mother never deserved the treatment she had received. Barbie remembered the hours of labour her mother had put in to make the car payments when her father was in the Air Force. Barbie's voice rang loud and clear: "You can leave if you want, but you can't take the car. Mother paid for it."

Harry raised his arm high as if to strike her. Then he dropped it and walked out of the house. Harry never left home, nor did he speak of Barbie's reaction. It was a rare event for Barbie to rebel although she often became angry and disappeared to the woodpile to work off the excess energy that her wrath produced.

The woodpile stood in the backyard. Harry split the wood and piled one stick upon another in a circle. Into the centre of the circle he, or the children, threw the other cut-up sticks. Here Barbie fled to reduce stress and anger by heaving the wood with all the force she could muster. She wanted to be like her kind, gentle mother and not filled with negative emotions. She held in her mind the words spoken to her, "If you are half the woman your mother is when you grow up, you will be a great woman."

For many years Harry hired a man to help him in the garage. One of the family's favourites was a young man named Roy. As a little boy Roy had stood watching Harry as he worked and said, "Someday I'm going to be a garage man like Harry." When he became a teen, he approached Harry and was hired.

Suddenly the house came alive with song and laughter especially when Harry wasn't home. Roy sang and played the guitar and all the teens joined in and coaxed him for more.

After a while Roy said, "That's enough. I'm going for a walk."

Soon after Joyce said, "I have to go and mail a letter at the post office," and away she went. Within a few days the family noticed that this happened every night. Roy and Joyce had fallen in love and were meeting in secret.

Harry started getting restless again. He sold the garage and bought a general store. Verta stood behind the counter supporting her husband and interacting with respect and consideration with each customer. Sometimes the children took turns selling in the store. Harry instilled solid business values in his family: *The customer is always right. Greet the customer with a smile.* Other values were caught, not taught; such as, *Honesty is the Best Policy*, *Quality Pays*, and *Expect to Give and Receive Dignity.*

Some of the patrons belonged to the First Nations. Verta had learned to respect them, as she often picked them up in the taxi and drove them to their destinations. She was often heard to say, "Sometimes white men make passes at me, but never an Indian."

A government ruling that people of First Nations could not buy any products with alcohol in them caused Verta, Harry, and family some concern for their First Nations friends. Some products, including pure vanilla, had to be hidden from view.

In her second year of High School the teacher approached Barbie one day. "The teacher of the Middle School is going on leave tomorrow for her father's funeral. Would you like to sub for her?"

Barbie's eyes lit up. She had always wanted to be a teacher.

The next day bright and early she was at the Middle School greeting each of the grades three, four, and five children, and when she rang the bell they all filed in.

Little brother, Petie, sat in the middle of a row. His bright blue eyes shone and his sister wondered what mischief he was planning, but the day went well except for one incident that caught Barbie off guard.

She had been instructed that when she went home for lunch, the children were to play outside and she was to lock the classroom. Barbie obeyed but when she came back after lunch a sudden shower had drenched the children. She lit the classroom heater and tried to dry and warm them. She determined not to be defeated by any situation.

Barbie's grade ten year was a great success for her in other ways too. Academically she excelled. Her favourite subject was Algebra. She thought of it as fun and games, and like a detective she solved the problems without much effort. Soon the teacher asked her to help some of the students in a higher grade, and also arranged for her to take two years of algebra in one year. That proved to be a bit more challenging and occasionally a neighbour tutored her.

"That girl has talent," the neighbour said to Harry. "You must send Barbie to university."

"No, I will not," said Harry. "She's a female. She'll just get married and waste all my money."

No matter how persuasive the neighbour became, Harry remained adamant and he said to Barbie, "After you finish this year, I'll only give you one more year of schooling."

Barbie took her father at his word. She wanted to be a teacher but one more year was not enough education to achieve that goal. She never considered persuasion. Her father had always been a man whose word was final, so she began to strategize.

"If you'll send me to business school next year, Dad, then I will be able to get a job and support myself," she said.

So Barbie enrolled in Little's Business College in Dauphin, a nearby town. She was to start school in September. The president/owner, Mr. Little, promised to get her and the other students a job upon completion of the course.

The old woman pondered Barbie's interrupted education. Perhaps that was why Barbie always had a lust for learning, and was never satisfied with the status quo. One time she challenged a course and passed; other times she took college courses or other training. One of her many mottoes became "Lifelong Learning."

Much happened in the little family before September though. Harry decided to build a kitchen on to the back of their house. They had only a small dirt cellar but now Harry hired workers to dig a full-sized basement under the planned addition.

One morning just after the basement was dug, Barbie was eating breakfast when she noticed something strange. She turned to Roy who had also risen early and said, "Look out the kitchen window. Water is running across the road. That's odd." They alerted the family as water continued to advance. The river that usually resembled a lazy stream had flooded and was advancing towards their house. Soon there was almost a foot of water around their area of the village. It was a warm June day and almost the last of the school season so classes were dismissed. Barbie and all the older children took off their shoes and socks and waded in the pleasant water.

Other effects of the flood were not pleasant though. Water flowed into the newly dug basement and Harry feared that the whole house would slide into the hole.

When the waters receded mud caked the road, covered the gardens, and tracked into the house.

Finally the basement and kitchen were finished but Verta was ill. She was sent to Winnipeg and underwent a gall bladder operation as her life held in the balance.

While she was in hospital, Harry painted the kitchen in his spare time. Barbie watched him as he turned his worry into a work of love. He painted the kitchen white with red trim ready for his wife when she returned home.

Finally she was released from the hospital. Still very weak and ill, she took the train in Winnipeg and arrived at the train station at two a.m. She looked around but Harry had not come to meet her although he had been informed of her arrival time. In desperation she asked the station master to take her home. Verta saw this as an indication of his disregard for her, yet Barbie observed his love and worry during her illness. His relation to both his wife and his children was a strange mixture of affection, control, and disrespect.

The old woman blinked tears from her eyes, and wiped her nose as she recalled Verta's pain, and Barbie's inability to understand her father's behaviour.

In retrospect, the old woman mused, Barbara was only partially right when she said her mother had paid for the car. While her father was in the Air Force, Verta had carefully taken money each month from the military wife's allowance to make the car payment. When he was discharged he picked up the responsibility.

Barbie and her family were jubilant. It was near the end of the school year, May 8, 1945, that victory was declared in Europe. People nicknamed it VE Day (Victory in Europe).

On August 15th, 1945, Harry, Verta, and Barbie were visiting friends in the countryside when they received the news: The allies had defeated the Japanese armies. Barbie had no conception of the damage that the atomic bombs had caused as they fell on Nagasaki and Hiroshima. She just knew that the war was over. So many people had sacrificed; so many people had been wounded or died, and she was glad the danger had passed.

As horrific as the war had been, life continued without a blip for Barbie. She was to start Business College in September, and was ready and poised to start adult life as an independent woman; or so she thought.

Chapter Seven

Barbie's Adventures

The old woman decided. Today was the day she would resume Barbie's story. Her husband had been ill for more than a month and Barbie's story had lain unopened. The old woman knew that Barbie would not care, for Barbie believed people were more important than stories, even true ones.

Still, Barbie's story tugged at her like a little child impatient to be heard. But wait. First she had to take her morning stroll.

The old woman put on her coat and gloves and stepped outside. The air was damp and crisp with fall. As she stepped forward, the chimes that hung in the porch rang as she brushed against them. She paused as she listened to the caw of a crow, the cheep of a little bird, and the scolding of a squirrel as it cautioned her not to steal his walnuts.

Crumpled yellow-brown leaves carpeted the lawn chairs and the sandbox where toys sat idle. Memories flooded her of generations of children that had played in that sandbox under that tree. But Barbie had not been one of them. She had her own adventures.

Barbie moved into the home of a landlady named Ethel who lived with her elderly father and mother. Besides her clothing Barbie took her brand-new watch. It was the first one she had ever owned. Harry and Verta bought it for her eighteenth birthday. She needed it to time her typing and shorthand. Barbie also took her guitar with her.

She wanted to play music and the missionary's wife had given her some lessons on her own piano, but now Barbie was living in the next town. She decided to learn how to play the guitar, so at the first opportunity she enrolled in lessons.

Every weekday Barbie walked to the Business College. It took her about twenty-five minutes each morning and again at night. So in rain, sleet, or snow she set out to walk. Barbie enjoyed walking. In her childhood she and her friend Lena often walked on the railroad tracks. It seemed safe to them as the tracks were on level ground and they had lots of time and opportunity to get off them when they heard the train whistle. Sometimes Barbie walked alone on the road for a couple of miles. She particularly liked to walk in a stiff prairie breeze as she battled and won against the winds that buffeted her.

In the evenings Barbie practised shorthand or guitar, went to a church meeting, or to a guitar lesson. She had no typewriter so she could only type at school. Usually she caught the train home on the weekends.

Whenever Barbie returned from College tired and hungry, Ethel had a wonderful meal ready. Her mother also had a talent for cooking. Her biscuits, pies, butter tarts, and cream puffs were prize winners. The only problem was that between working in the store and driving the taxi she had little or no time to cook. Meals were often quickly warmed up potatoes and a bit of meat or cheese from the grocery store. Now, Barbie revelled in Ethel's cooked meals ready and waiting for her. All of her life to now, Barbie had been skinny, her arms and legs resembling long match sticks. Little by little with Ethel's meals she started to gain weight.

Barbie sat in a restaurant while her Dad and Mom ordered a dinner for her. They had asked Ethel to join them as a treat for her faithful care of their daughter. Barbie ate with gusto as she had no money to dine out. After dinner she said, "Thanks Dad. I really enjoyed that. It's a long time since I had a good meal."

Barbie stammered as her face turned red, she had meant a good *restaurant* meal. She didn't know how to undo her thoughtless words.

One morning Barbie was typing in the classroom when one of the other students came in late. He turned to her and said, "Woof. Up she went."

Barbie gave him a look of incomprehension and he added, "Your Dad's store burned to the ground last night." For a second she sat stunned, then asked the teacher to be excused and walked across the street to the telephone office.

"I'll phone the store," Barbie said to herself. "There must be a mistake. Someone will answer my call." She walked into a booth at the telephone office and informed the operator to call the number. There was no answer. The operator came on the line and said, "Would you like to talk to the Ochre River telephone operator?"

When the operator came on the line, she told Barbie all the details of the fire that had destroyed their family's store. Although a hired man had temporarily been caught in the conflagration, everyone had managed to get out safely.

Just the weekend before, Barbie had admired all the Christmas merchandise that had come in. She could not rid her mind of all the children's muffs meant to keep small hands warm. On the front of each one was a beautiful doll's head. Although Barbie had never played with dolls, she admired the cute muffs and imagined all the little girls who would be excited to receive them on Christmas morning. Now the muffs were just piles of ashes.

On the weekend Barbie went to see her parents. She noticed that her Dad had set aside his despair and jumped into action. "We will clear out the front room of our house, bring in more merchandise and set up the store there. People will still be able to get rationed items."

One Friday four months after she began Business College the president said to her, "Barbara, I want you to meet the manager of the Bank of Nova Scotia, here in Dauphin. Be there prompt at nine o'clock Monday morning. He's hiring a stenographer. You're ready for the position."

Barbie spent the weekend at her parents' home. Her Dad promised to drive her to the appointment. She awoke early and looked out the window. A prairie blizzard drove the snow in swirls and then formed banks. After breakfast she climbed into the car beside her father to drive the twenty miles. In normal weather they would have had plenty of time, but every mile or so Harry's car stopped and he had to get out and shovel the snow drifts off the road.

Finally nervous and exhausted from worry, Barbie arrived at the appointment. After the interview she went to the Business College where she received a reprimand for being late for a job application. Despite the hardships of the day, Barbie had been hired.

Although the pay was low even for that post-war period, her Dad told her that the job held prestige. Her wage was to be $55 dollars per month, plus a living-away allowance of $11. Board and room took a great deal of her wage and left her very little over for personal spending.

The bank staff welcomed her the next morning when she checked in for work. The manager seemed intimidating, while the accountant looked so stiff that a prairie wind might have broken him in two. She wondered if he ever smiled. She was shown her desk with an Underwood typewriter, a steno pad, a pencil, and a box of stamps to mail letters. "Bring your little pad in, Miss Pouncy," the manager said to Barbie. "You may as well begin." Barbie wrote the letter in shorthand as the manager dictated and blew smoke across the desk in her direction.

"That will be all for now. Go and type that for me to sign." Barbie was dismissed.

Barbie sat at her desk and studied her shorthand. She could easily read the body of the letter but couldn't decipher the name.

Frightened to return to the manager and reveal her failure, Barbie walked over to the First Teller and said, "Can you help me? Do you know this name?"

A smile of gratitude lit up Barbie's face as the teller gave her the answer. Barbie had learned her lesson. After that she always wrote the name in longhand.

Barbie tried to be the compliant stenographer. Her heart threatened to fail her a few times. On one occasion the bank examiner came, and after examining all the ledger books he came and checked her stamp account. She was a few pennies out. As she tried to assess his stern attitude, she had trouble determining if this was a serious matter or not. Another time a prairie breeze snatched some of the incoming correspondence from her as she walked down the street. A bystander helped her gather up every piece and Barbie said, "Thank you." Despite her embarrassment Barbie continued to learn about the work world.

The decision that Harry made to operate the store in their home was short-lived. He soon bought an unused barn, moved it on the store site, cleaned and remodelled it, and then reopened the store.

One early Monday morning Barbie crawled into the back seat of her Dad's Hudson car along with several crates of eggs her father was taking to Dauphin. Roy was sitting beside her Dad as he drove.

Several miles into their trip, Barbie noticed that the car was turning towards the road that led to the airport. *Why is Dad going in to the airport?* No sooner had Barbie asked herself the question than she noticed that the car was not turning into the airport but heading for the ditch. Part of the steering mechanism had failed. They later found out that the end of the tie rod had broken.

Barbie sat there unhurt. She pushed away the egg crates that had slid towards her and reached over to Roy in the front passenger seat. He was crying out in pain.

"Don't be silly, Roy," Barbie said. "You can't be hurt." With that, she leaned over the seat and picked up his leg that had been wedged between the two front seats. *Crunch…it was broken badly.* Barbie felt sick and knew she had been insensitive. Her actions were hurtful to her dear friend and prospective brother-in-law.

Barbie's father, who had suffered broken ribs, opened the door and walked to the airport office, still manned although the war had ended. Help arrived and Roy was transported to hospital where he spent weeks recovering from his severely fractured femur.

Joyce's eyes twinkled and a smile lit up her face as she said, "Roy and I are engaged. We're getting married in May."

Everyone in the family was excited. They all loved Roy.

The month of May arrived and Joyce was ecstatic. Her marriage to Roy was fast approaching. Ever practical, she decided to marry in a rosy-red suit. Bridesmaid Barbie was to wear a moss-green suit (suitable to wear to work later), and Faith who was the second bridesmaid was to wear a gold colour suit.

Roy was still on crutches but he had one big goal. He determined to walk unaided down the aisle of the community hall to marry his sweetheart.

Family and friends decorated the hall, and prepared dainty little sandwiches and tasty sweets to be served at the reception to follow the wedding.

"Run home," Verta said to Petie. (The house was only a block away.) "I forgot some things." After giving him a list she turned to finish another task. A half hour later she glanced outside to see Petie returning; driving the car! He was only twelve and still small for his age. He could barely see over the steering wheel but dared almost anything. He frequently questioned himself: "*Will I get away with this? Will I get a spanking? Is the pleasure worth the punishment?*" This time he figured it was well worth the risk. He had always wanted to drive and they were too busy to punish him.

The wedding was about to begin. Roy walked toward the front. Partway there he deposited his crutches and finished the journey unaided. Joyce, though usually shy, beamed with joy as she walked up the aisle with her father, followed by her two bridesmaids. She was finally marrying her best friend.

Harry had made up his mind. Joyce and Roy were married, and Barbie was independent. It was time for the rest of the family to move on. He had always hated the cold of the prairies and longed for warmer climate. "We're moving to British Columbia," he said to Verta. "Start packing. I've put the house and store up for sale. We'll go as soon as they sell."

Verta hated the move. She was leaving half her family behind but her husband had always been boss and she felt powerless. Once again, she put aside her own wishes and started to pack. It wasn't long after the wedding that she drove the two children, Faith and Petie, along with some possessions, over the many roads to B.C. Harry led the way in a truck carrying a load of furniture. "We are not stopping anywhere! We are driving straight through!" Harry said to Verta "Just follow me."

Verta followed; over the flat prairies, and the windy roads of the Big Bend; a dangerous gravel highway in the Rocky Mountains. (The Roger's Pass had not yet opened.) After days her eyes started to ache and she thought she was going blind but Harry kept travelling and she followed.

At last they arrived at their destination—a little fruit farm in the shelter of a big black rock in Vernon, B.C., located in the heart of the Okanagan Valley. Verta settled down to be a farmer's wife, mother of two dependent children, and pined for the two daughters she had left behind.

Mother and father had left, and Barbie walked into the empty house, not yet occupied by the buyers. Her heart felt bereft and as empty as the house. That night she slept there on a pad and in the daytime visited the new bride and groom. When the day was over she returned to Dauphin and resumed life there.

Once more Barbie fell into a routine: work, church, guitar practice and lessons, and writing a weekly letter to her Mom and Dad. She became close friends with some church people, but there were none her age.

The summer was drawing to a close and it was Barbie's nineteenth birthday. Ethel promised her a special dinner with a birthday cake. Barbie went off to work with anticipation. The day passed like a snail, but work was not going well.

As stenographer, it was Barbie's job to post the mail at the end of each day. In the outgoing mail there was a bank statement to Head Office that gave the details of the day's balances. As often happened, the Second Teller had trouble balancing her books. It fell to Barbie to help her. Although it was not in Barbie's (non-existent) job description, the logic was that she could not mail the bank statement until the books were balanced. So she toiled on. After a thirteen-hour day and no hope of overtime pay, she dropped the statement in the mail, and feeling sorry for herself she went home to a disappointed landlady and a reheated birthday dinner.

The old woman stopped typing on the computer, and walked to the window. Clouds gathered and she saw a patch of sunshine to the west. Harry thought Barbie was set for life. Though the pay was low and the hours sometimes long, he told her that it was a job with honour and prestige. But was it right for Barbie? Would Barbie stay in a job that failed to excite her, or would she dare to risk?

Chapter Eight

The Dare

Barbie greeted Mr. Shunk, the guest speaker at the church. He represented Winnipeg Bible Institute. "Barbara," he said, "Why don't you come to Bible School?"

"I can't afford it," Barbie said.

"Where is your faith?" said Mr. Shunk.

Barbie stood still and said nothing. *Where indeed was her faith? She believed in God and she knew he would protect her. She had always wanted to study the Bible and learn more about God and now was her chance.*

She looked at Mr. Shunk. "I have $82 dollars in my Savings Account. How do I start?"

"Well," he said. "Tuition for the first semester is $50 and you will have to pay train fare. When you arrive in Winnipeg, we will match you up with a family and they will give you board and room and a small amount of spending money and you will work for them after school and Saturdays.

Without a backward thought, Barbie gave notice at work, paid the tuition fees, packed her clothes in a big trunk, and bought a train ticket. She left the guitar behind, never to be picked up again.

Ah, Winnipeg, with its wide avenues and the Golden Boy on top of the domed roof of the parliament buildings. During one of her previous trips to Winnipeg she had visited the legislative buildings. She stood in awe of its majesty and marvelled at the Blue Room, a room furbished completely in various shades of blue. But now Barbie had only one goal: to get to school and find her new home.

Barbie arrived at the school with her trunk and its few belongings inside. Immediately she met Mrs. Green, who had arranged with the school to hire Barbie upon arrival, and together they travelled to her apartment.

Soon Barbie adjusted to her work schedule. When she arrived home from school each day she helped make supper for the family. After supper she did the dishes and cleaned up the area. On Saturday she did housecleaning all day, as well as prepared meals. Sunday was a free day and she could come and go as she pleased. In return for her work, she received free board and room and $15 a month; mostly spent on bus fare, and personal toiletries. There was nothing left for pop or milk shakes, but since Barbie had never indulged in these extras she didn't miss them.

One day when she and Mrs. Green's daughter, Marie, were home alone together, Marie mentioned that Barbie was their maid. Barbie never thought of it that way. In her mind she was merely making money to pay for her schooling. Her Dad had always given the impression that not money or possessions, but place was important in life. Somehow, as poor as the family had been, Barbie always stood tall and unashamed.

The old woman recalled this time in Barbie's life. When Harry heard the news that his daughter had quit her job, moved to Winnipeg, attended Bible School, and supported herself by working as a maid he said, "Verta, I'm angry. I won't write to her. She had a perfectly good job and she quit, and for what? Don't you dare send her money."

Verta, unhappy but submissive, kept Harry's anger from Barbie, who for more than a year was not even aware of her father's antagonism although she might have guessed; her Dad had never allowed her to go to Christian camps and only tolerated church attendance. But she was too focused on her new life to notice. Besides, her mother faithfully wrote every week and gave her all the family news. In Barbie's mind she had made the decision and expected no help from her parents. She was an adult now. She took responsibility for her decisions.

School felt like heaven on earth. Barbie had respected God and Christian things all her life and now she immersed herself in friendships and the studies that fascinated her.

One of the most important lessons she learned that year was that God supplies needs. One of the first problems occurred when Barbie discovered that she needed a black dress whenever the school choir sang in public. She did not own a black dress nor did her meager allowance stretch so that she might buy one.

One day at lunch time her friend Louisa said, "Barbara, are you willing to skip lunch? The Bay has a sale of black dresses for $5 and I'd like you to go with me and look at them."

Away Louisa and Barbie went. When at The Bay she had Barbie try on a black dress and then paid for it and handed it to her. Number one prayer was answered.

Sometimes Barbie would put a hand in her coat pocket and find $2 or $5. God's messengers were helping.

It was less than a month till Christmas and Barbie wanted to send her family some gifts. She looked through her puny possessions and found some cotton fabric, some embroidery thread and with these she made a couple of dresser-top runners; one for her mother and one for her sister. With a little out of her monthly pay she bought her Dad a twenty-five cent jigsaw puzzle and a game for Pete. She wrapped the parcel and sent it.

When Barbie's Dad saw the presents he said, "How pitiful. Verta, aren't you sneaking her a bit of money?"

"No," said Verta, "you told me not to."

That whole year poverty nipped at Barbie's heels, but through it all she developed a trust in God. Christmas holidays arrived and Barbie had saved just enough to take the train to visit her sister Joyce and new husband, Roy. As she was leaving the school to catch the train one of the male students, Dave (a giant of a man) said, "May I see you off at the train station?"

Standing at the wicket with Dave by her side, Barbie laid down her ticket money. "Oh, that's not enough," said the station attendant. "The fare's been raised."

Barbie stood speechless as she wondered what to do. She had used her last penny on the ticket and she was two dollars short. Quietly, Ben laid down a $2 bill and said, "Merry Christmas, Barbie." God through one of his people had come through once more.

Mrs. Green became ill, and she, Marie, and Barbie all moved to the outskirts of Winnipeg to the home of her son, Dr. Green. Barbie admired her new boss, Mrs. Green, Jr., who was also a medical doctor. She never felt like *just a maid,* but was always treated with dignity and respect. Transportation to and from Bible School was by streetcar and bus. She walked the half mile from home to the streetcar terminal where she got on, rode for quite a long time, transferred to a bus, and finally arrived at the school.

One day she realized that she would run out of streetcar tickets by payday. What would she do? Pray, of course. Soon after that, the dear old family gardener approached her and said, "Barbie, I'd like you to have these." He handed her a book of streetcar tickets.

Another time, Thursday came and Barbie wrote her usual letter to her mother, but she had no four cent stamps left. The letter would have to wait, unless…*"Well, God, is it too small a matter to pray for a stamp—you know mother will worry if she doesn't hear from me."* When she arrived home after school, Mrs. Green handed her a letter that had come in the mail. Barbie opened it. The letter was from her former landlady, Ethel, and she pulled out (you guessed right) a book of stamps.

The old woman paused in her story. Barbie had never before or after the event received either a book of streetcar tickets or a book of stamps. And the amazing fact was that she never received the streetcar tickets when she needed stamps or stamps when she needed streetcar tickets. She received exactly what she needed, when she needed it. And while time faded the memories of textbook lessons learned, she never forgot the many miraculous provisions.

Barbie's money problems were far from over. One day she was walking down the street with a fellow student, Ken. They had a special friendship and she felt free to share her concerns with him, although she knew he had no means to help her. The second semester tuition fees were soon due, and Barbie didn't have money to pay them. "Ken, if I only had $80 I would be okay," she said. Someone else was listening to that conversation. It was God.

Shortly after, she received a letter from her uncle in England. "Barbara," he said, "your aunt has received a small legacy in the United States and instead of sending it to us, we have asked them to send it to you to help in your schooling."

The gift arrived shortly. It wasn't much but added to her pay check it equalled $80. Once more Barbie marvelled at God's provision through people of goodwill.

In March, the Red River that bordered the back of Green's property started to break up. Huge ice floes piled up and vied for place as they fought down the river. Barbie stared with a look of wonderment on her face. The meandering stream that wound its way through her childhood haunts at Ochre River held no such marvels.

April arrived and the end of Barbie's first year of Bible School. Mrs. Green asked her to continue working full-time in the summer. Her job entailed occasional care of the baby boy, cleaning house, making meals, washing dishes, and baking desserts. Mrs. Green gave her a cookbook and said, "Barbara, I'd like you to go through the book in order and bake one new recipe every day." What an idea! Barbie loved to cook, more than any other household chores. Everyday held some special delicacy.

One day, she made an apple pie. Although she had baked for her family before she left home, she had never tackled a pie. The crust was thick and had ugly cracks in it; nevertheless, the family enjoyed eating it and Mrs. Green encouraged her to try again.

One day in May, Barbie opened the telegram with trembling fingers. It said, "Baby girl arrived. Stop. Joyce and baby fine. Stop. Roy." Her face shining with excitement, Barbie asked Mrs. Green if she could have a few days off, and soon was on the train to see her very first niece.

Barbie held the infant as a love that she had never fully experienced welled up inside her. Too soon the visit ended, and she saw the baby only in her dreams until Christmas holidays and her next visit.

In September, it was almost time for Barbie to start year two of Bible School. One day, Mrs. Green, Jr., who was pregnant with her second child, said, "Barbie, I like your work but I need full-time help now."

So Barbie went to see her professor, Mr. Shunk, who had originally placed her with the Green family. He sent a lady to the Green residence to interview her. "As my maid, Barbara, you will wear a uniform with an apron and cap. You are to let me know if you'll accept this job."

Something in Barbie's heart went dead. *Wear a uniform? A maid's uniform?* The woman had seemed distant and uncaring and Barbie dreaded the idea of working for her. As she went about her job, Mrs. Green Jr., noticed her lack of joy. "You don't want that job, do you? Well, don't take it then. Something else will turn up."

Before Barbie had time to be concerned, Mrs. Green has arranged for her to work for board, room and $20 a month at her aunt and uncle's home. Soon Barbie packed her few belongings and went to the home of her new employers, Mr. and Mrs. Wesley.

Mrs. Wesley was tall and slim with a hearing impairment. When someone rang the doorbell, a light blinked to alert her; the same happened when the telephone rang. Mr. Wesley was a kindly man who on rare occasions gave Barbie a bit of extra spending money.

Barbie's bedroom was in the basement and she enjoyed her study and sleeping quarters. And so a new year started, and Barbie quickly adjusted to new employers and the second year of studies and friendships with a wide variety of people.

Ken and Barbie were becoming closer friends, and as New Year's Day approached he invited her to his parents' home for the celebration. She was excited to meet his family but a day before he said, "Barbie, instead of going to my place, I am taking you to a restaurant for a meal. My mother has refused to have an English girl in her home."

Barbie understood Ken's dilemma. She just had to think of her father's reaction to people of the German race: "The only good German is a dead one." The war between Germany and England had just finished and enmity prevailed between the races. While Ken was Dutch, rather than German, she knew that her father would respond negatively to her friendship with him.

On New Year's Day, Ken rang the doorbell and in his hand he held a long-stemmed rose, the first flower that anyone had ever given Barbie. She didn't know the right thing to do with the rose. Did she carry it with her for the evening or put it in water? So she put it in water. Then they went and enjoyed their time together and tried to forget their parents' race issues.

Both Barbie and Ken received good grades in exams, but Barbie wondered if she should try to lower her marks so that he would always feel superior to her. She pondered the question but finally decided that she had to be honest to herself and do her best, whatever the outcome to their friendship.

The school year came to a close and her mother had arranged for Barbie to come home for the summer and work for a neighbour. So Barbie boarded a train to British Columbia. The train lumbered along the prairies and by nightfall it had passed Calgary, Alberta, and entered the foothills. "Ah, the mountains," Barbie whispered to herself, "the beautiful mountains." Then she fell asleep in her berth in the sleeper car, all the other travelers fast asleep in theirs.

About 3 a.m. Barbie roused enough to look out the window of the sleeper. "Wow," she said out loud, unconscious of the sleeping people around her. The train hugged the huge mountain as it wound around and around, and Barbie craned her neck to see the top of it. Fascinated she watched as enormous mountains seemed to pass before her wondering eyes. She had seen calendar pictures of mountains but somehow they had seemed like figments of the artist's imagination. These mountains were real and amazing.

Finally, Barbie fell asleep. She dreamed of a land of mountains, valleys, and lakes—a place where her parents lived but she had never seen before—the beautiful Okanagan Valley.

Chapter Nine

A Land Flowing with Milk and Honey

Too excited to sleep for long, Barbie watched the moving landscape. Huge ice-capped, rocky mountains towered as the train wove its tortuous way round and round. At one point she watched the train emerge, as the caboose entered the spiralling tunnels.

After some time the mountains became shorter and the valley became somewhat wider. As Barbie waited to transfer to another train in Sicamous, B.C., pesky mosquitoes buzzed around her head. The Canadian Pacific train to which she transferred rumbled on through the North Okanagan Valley. She noted a little town called Armstrong, where the railway went through the middle of the town. It sat in the valley between the rolling hills. Ten minutes out of Armstrong, the hills were covered with apple blossoms in full bloom. Other than the mighty mountains, she had never seen such a glorious view before.

The conductor said "Vernon, B.C," as the train lumbered to a stop, and Barbie stepped into another world; or so it seemed to her.

Barbie's mother, who had greeted her at the train depot, drove her through Vernon, down a steep hill called Black Rock to a little farm at the base of it. Barbie marvelled at the blossoming fruit trees in the yard and enjoyed a reunion with her family. She had not seen them for two years and although her life had been full, she had missed them—especially her dear mother.

Barbie had little time for reminiscing though, for she needed to work and earn money for the next year. Soon she met Mr. and Mrs. Hunter, and an aging mother: Mrs. Hunter, Sr.

Mrs. Hunter, Sr. had just returned from hospital. Barbie's employers told her that their mother was very ill and she must watch her all night and call them if she became worse. She was shown a closet off the bedroom that held a chair and a light by which Barbie could read or work on some project.

Barbie sat in her little cubby-hole reading a book and glancing at the old woman as she slept. Finally, her tired eyes forced her to quit and she sat thinking. Night after night the same happened until one night she awakened to hear Mr. Hunter say, "Did you fall asleep, Barbara?"

"Sorry, Mr. Hunter, I guess I must have dozed off."

"That okay, Barbara, I think it's time to change your job. Mother's health has improved. How about helping around the house and doing a few chores for me for the rest of the summer?"

Barbie loved the old lady but she was glad of the change of duties, as well as an understanding boss.

Each day she had to pump water for the chickens and gather eggs. She soon learned the routine: Grab the wire egg bucket, set it on the stand, grab the pump handle and start the flow of water. As the water came out of the spout, she watched it run into a series of troughs until it reached a holding area from which the chickens could drink. When she had finished pumping water, she grabbed her empty egg pail and set off to gather eggs in the hen house.

One day as she followed her routine, a man walked by on the road, "You'll never carry water in that bucket," he laughed. It took her a second to realize that he thought her egg bucket with its many holes was meant to carry water (or was he joking; she never knew).

During the summer her parents sold the little farm at the foot of Black Rock and moved into Vernon. Their new house was a two-storey building and her Dad rented a service station, while Barbie continued to work at the Hunter farm.

One of the frequent visitors to the household was Ted, a soldier at the Army Camp. He was about Barbie's age and a family friend whom she enjoyed having around. One day she wrote to her boyfriend, Ken, and mentioned Ted. In retrospect it probably caused a rift in their friendship.

The rift became wider when Ken asked to come out and visit her family. "I don't think that would be wise," Barbie said. She cared deeply about Ken, but she knew her father might be rude to him. Ken was a very spiritual man with a different ethnic background. While her father's religious background was in the Church of England, he seemed agnostic in his approach to God.

Nevertheless, when Barbie was asked to speak at the local church, her father attended. After the service he said to her, "Barb, that was interesting; you're very idealistic." Barbie never knew whether it was faint praise or veiled criticism.

The old woman paused to think of Barbie's relationship with her father. At some level Barbara disliked his autocratic ways. On another level she wanted his approval although not at the expense of herself: her beliefs in God or her self-determination. She wanted to be independent, to stand tall and reach out to God and to others in love and friendship. Barbie had no desire to live her adult life subservient to her father. But at some level the old woman knew that Barbie loved her Dad—always did, and always would.

Chapter Ten

THE PROBLEM YEAR

The summer fled like a jet in flight as the Train Conductor yelled, "Winnipeg!" and Barbie poised to start her final year of Bible School training.

Once more she earned her board and room by working as a mother's helper. The household consisted of Mrs. Ford, her nine-year-old son Thomas, four-year Danny, and an absent husband who was a touring businessman.

School had just begun when Ken said, "Barbie, I'd like to take you out for a drive one evening when you get off work."

This was a rare occasion because life was busy for both Barbie and Ken. So she looked forward to it with anticipation. However, as they were driving, Ken told her he had decided to break up with her. He laid no blame on her but she knew deep down that she had driven a couple of nails in the coffin of their relationship. Tears flowed freely as he slowly drove Barbie home.

At her new home Barbie adjusted to the household and to college life. One day Mrs. Ford said, "Barbara, you need to know that I am an alcoholic. You don't need to worry because I belong to Alcoholics Anonymous. I haven't taken a drink in a long time."

Barbie put the thought in the back of her mind. Mrs. Ford was doing a great job as a mother and homemaker, although Barbie was somewhat aware of the dangers of drinking.

The only time she remembered alcohol in her childhood home was one time when she had experienced a series of colds and her father decided she should drink some brandy mixed with water. She hated the taste and gagged. So her Dad stopped forcing her and she never was tempted to drink.

Some of her uncles and aunts drank a great deal of alcohol and she never liked what it did to her beloved relatives. Her Mom grieved over its effects and warned her children to avoid alcohol.

Studies carried on and Barbie's life was full with friends and studies in faith. Still pressures arose that she had never experienced before.

She was chosen as editor of the school's yearbook with Miss Allan as teacher overseer. Pressures to perform, the break-up of her relationship with Ken, some minor problems with Miss Allan, combined with the insistence of a young man to become his girlfriend when she had no romantic interest in him, all combined to create a year of friction.

One day when Barbie returned from school she found Mrs. Ford in bed. "I have the flu," she said. So Barbie carried on preparing meals, cleaning the house, and caring for the boys.

Day after day Mrs. Ford's condition remained the same. "Perhaps you should see a doctor," Barbie said.

"Oh, I'll be okay, Barbara. No need to worry."

But despite Mrs. Ford's reassurances Barbie became alarmed. One day she smelled alcohol as she neared her employer. *"Perhaps she is taking something for her flu,"* said Barbie to herself and carried on with her duties.

Problems increased as Barbie came home to find that Mrs. Ford had attempted to wash laundry. The wet clothes were tangled in the stalled wringer of the washing machine, and the stairway was charred indicating that she had extinguished a fire.

Alarm bells rang in Barbie's mind. Mrs. Ford did not have influenza. This was related to her alcohol problem. She said to her boss, "Mrs. Ford, you must get help or Children's Welfare authorities will come and take your children."

"Don't worry, Barbara, I am quitting drinking today. I have learned my lesson."

So Barbie went off to school. She knew the stress affected her. *Were Thomas and little Danny safe? What should she do? But Mrs. Ford had made a promise, maybe she would keep it; she loved her children.*

So began Barbie's quiet quest to rid the house of alcohol. She found bottles in the bedposts in Mrs. Ford's room and quietly confiscated them. Sometimes she poured the alcohol down the drain in the basement and sometimes hid the bottles on a clothes closet shelf in her bedroom. She laid her hats on top of the bottles to camouflage them, and her employer never found them.

Barbie busied herself around the quiet house when she arrived home from college. One day someone knocked on the door. There stood a neighbour unknown to Barbie, "Mrs. Ford has had a car accident. She ran into a power pole in the back lane."

As Mrs. Ford shakily entered the house accompanied by Thomas and Danny, the neighbour quietly stood by the door. When he and Barbie were alone he said, "There's a case of beer in the car. What do you want me to do with it?"

"Get rid of it," Barbie said. "I don't care what you do with it. It mustn't come in this house."

Barbie knew that she didn't have any authority to make such decisions, but the situation was getting desperate. Just the day before, she had found a five dollar bill under the kitchen fridge. When she asked Thomas if he knew anything about it he said, "Yes, I hid it there. I thought we might run out of money and we'd need it to buy food."

During this time, Mr. Ford was away on a business trip and Mrs. Ford's mother, who usually oversaw her daughter's well-being in her husband's absence, was on an extended holiday. Barbie knew she had to act although she had no experience in dealing with such a dangerous situation.

The next morning at college Barbie said to the work placement teacher, "Mr. Shunk, I need to talk to you," and she poured out the whole story.

Relieved that she had taken action, Barbie went to classes. After school finished she went home. Visitors from Alcoholics Anonymous filled the house. Like a zombie, Barbie did what was necessary to care for the boys and look after the guests. One of them said, "Barbara, we have called a doctor to look after Mrs. Ford. He will be coming later on this evening."

When the doctor knocked at the door, Barbie was in the washroom vomiting, while Thomas was running down the stairs screaming. He had awoken frightened by a nightmare. As the doctor walked in the house he said, "And *who* is the patient here?"

The old woman stopped writing. Memories of Barbie's horrors tumbled one upon another. And she hadn't even described some of the most distressing: feces smeared over the toilet, gobs of peanut butter on the kitchen floor, and urine on the chesterfield. The memories of the damages alcohol had done to a beautiful woman, her wonderful children, and even to Barbie seared her mind.

But out of the experience the old woman knew that Barbie had developed an understanding of the disease, and a wonderful respect for the brave people of Alcohol Anonymous who rose from their own personal problems to help other people.

It was April and school was winding down, and Barbie received an invitation to live cost-free with a retired missionary. When Barbie told Mrs. Ford that she would be leaving her job early, Mrs. Ford said, "But, Barbara, I have scheduled minor surgery and I was counting on you to help."

So Barbie declined the offer of the missionary and carried on for the rest of the term. Although stress at home was alleviated, there was another stress. It came when she received a letter from her Dad saying that her precious mother had become ill. "As soon as school is out, Barbara, come home. Your mother is very ill and may be dying." Whenever the phone rang, Barbie tensed. *Was it a call from her father to tell her that her mother had died?*

Graduation day came and went. Barbie packed her few belongings in her big trunk and said "Goodbye" to her friends. Then she waited in the Winnipeg train station. The mighty Red River had flooded its banks, and Barbie saw pockets of sobbing people. They were crying because they left homes as waters poured into them. Finally, the train rolled in and Barbie mentally said goodbye to Winnipeg and three glorious (well, almost glorious) years of studies in God's word, and to her Bible School friends of faith.

When the train conductor came to collect the tickets, he informed the passengers that they were being rerouted to Saskatoon because of the flood, and there would be a lay-over there for a couple of hours. As she settled down to enjoy the trip, a handsome, tall, brown-eyed young man said to her, "My name is Norman Smith. I noticed that you were wearing a pin with letters on it."

"Oh," said Barbie, "I just graduated from Winnipeg Bible Institute, and that is my graduation pin. My name is Barbara Pouncy."

For the balance of the ride to Saskatoon, Norman and Barbie sat together and shared some things about their lives. Just before the train pulled into Saskatoon, they exchanged names and addresses, and as they walked off the train they said their goodbyes.

Barbie sat in the train station and then decided she would take a walk and see a little of the city. As she strolled along the streets window-shopping, she became aware that someone was following her. She tested her instincts. She slowed down, the steps behind her slowed; she walked faster and whoever was following her also sped up. She pretended not to notice but determined to return to the safety of the train station, where she waited until it was time to board the train.

As the train rumbled through the prairies and over the Rocky Mountains, Barbie put thoughts of school, work, and Ken behind her. It was now time to begin her new life in beautiful British Columbia.

Chapter Eleven

Life in Beautiful British Columbia

The wintry feel had almost gone when the old woman picked up her stick to walk along the farm trails. She felt the sun as it warmed her face and the spring breezes that gently caressed her. She saw three or four dandelions that had broken through the grass, and she noted the new leaves beginning to emerge from the branches of the old maple tree. Spring, glorious spring had arrived.

She thought once more of Barbie and the writing she had agreed to do for her son. Despite her advancing years, the old woman still remembered Barbie's dismay when her parents wrote that they had moved from Vernon to Armstrong, the little town where the railroad ran through the middle of it. She smiled knowingly. Barbie would come to love that little town.

The old woman's pen had lain idle as she dealt with various personal issues, but she reasoned: if it's going to be, it's up to me. No one else is going to tell Barbie's story. Besides, she didn't believe in doing half a job. So on with the task.

Barbie opened the door and walked into her parent's new house to see her precious mother. Evidence of her mother's brush with death was obvious to Barbie. Still, the table was set and from the oven emanated the smell of roasting chicken. Mom had always shown her love by cooking for her family, and Barbie had missed that unspoken demonstration of mother's love. Her father had bought a service garage, Terminal Motors, and would soon be home for supper. Faith was now a vivacious teenager almost ready to graduate from High School, and fun-loving Petie (who now insisted that people stop calling him by his nickname and call him by his real name: Frank) was fifteen but looked about twelve years old.

After supper and a visit with her family, the household settled down for the night, except for Barbie. Her reverie was interrupted when a knock came at the door, and there stood Norman Smith.

"Hello, Barbie," he said, "I don't want to lose you forever. I have fallen in love with you. Will you marry me?"

Wow, Barbie thought to herself, this is sudden. After a time of discussion, Barbie said, "I'm sorry, Norman. This is too fast. Let me have some time to think of it."

"No, Barbie, you have to decide now," said Norman.

Barbie shook her head, "Norman, although I like you, I will have to say no."

The old woman paused in her writing. Norman sure was a fast worker and for a while Barbie wondered whether or not she had made the right decision. He did seem nice, but she didn't really know him. The old woman knew that Barbie had shown wisdom in her decision; it's good to wait for the right person.

Life fell into place in Armstrong. Barbie helped her mother, and soon her Mom became well and strong.

"Mom," Barbie said, "I think it is time for me to get a job. My clothes are all worn and I want to be independent."

Barbie's first desire was to work in a church to use the knowledge and skills she had acquired. She sent applications to many churches but they were declined: they were looking for men, not women.

Then Barbie applied to get into an accounting program in which the participants were paid a stipend while learning on the job. Her math skills had been excellent in school and she thought she could put her aptitude to work. To her chagrin they said, "I'm sorry, Barbara. We only accept men."

It seemed to Barbie that she had experienced a lifetime of rejections because she was female. It began when her father referred to Petie as "his son and heir" and to his daughters as "only dishwashers."

Even at Bible School when they chose a valedictorian she was told that she would not be chosen because men had louder voices and could be heard in the large church auditorium.

Finally, Barbie decided to visit Aunt Emily and Uncle Howard, who lived in Cloverdale in the Fraser Valley, close to New Westminster, B.C. While there she would hunt for a job at the coast.

She enjoyed living with Aunt Emily, Uncle Howard, and their two girls, Elaine and Merle. Her aunt and Barbie had fun together. They enrolled in a home-nursing course, and often went bowling. But she knew there was more to life than fun and she really needed a job. Besides she might be a financial burden to her relatives who were not rich.

One day, Barbie discovered an ad that described a course that combined training with paid work and would lead to qualifications as a psychiatric nurse. She applied. Once more, after she filled out the application form she discovered that she failed a requirement; this time because she had not been a resident of British Columbia for two years.

She applied to B.C. Telephone Company as an operator. There were no openings at present but they would keep her name on file.

About that time, Uncle Howard and Aunt Emily moved into New Westminster. Now, Barbie's task of job-hunting began in earnest. One day she stood in a room packed with about seventy women all seeking a sales position in a new Zeller's store.

When they called out, "Barbara Pouncy," Barbie walked into a room.

"Welcome, Barbara," said the interviewer who introduced herself as the Personnel Manager. "What experience have you had as a sales clerk?"

"I worked for my Dad in his store," said Barbie.

A look of disinterest passed over the interviewer's face as she scanned Barbie's application, but it brightened as she read the final notes on the form. Under the heading: *Other Training,* Barbie had written "Business course at Dauphin Business College,"

"Can you type?'

"I haven't touched a typewriter for three years," said Barbie.

The interviewer said, "But is typing something you forget how to do?"

"No, I don't think so," said Barbie.

"Great," said the manager, "you're hired. You can start immediately. All female employees are required to wear good dresses; no skirts or blouses. You'll be working for me in the Personnel Department."

Barbie soon learned that she would be stationed in the Information Booth on the first floor of the unfinished department store. As young women came to inquire about a job, she provided the first screening. If the girl was not clean or appropriately groomed, Barbie had to send her away. Other application forms were accepted and an appointment with the manager was scheduled.

Barbie enjoyed this job. Construction workers sometimes dropped by the booth and joked, "Will you give me a date?" or some other nonsensical question. They only got a smile from her as she quietly went about her work.

Finally, the hiring process completed, construction finished, the store stocked, announcements in the paper, and the doors were opened.

Barbie had never seen anything like it. People pushed and shoved through the doors in order to get to the sale-specials before anyone else. One woman in the crowd walked right through a glass panel beside the door. Cut and bleeding, she was rushed to First Aid, while an employee cleaned up the glass. Finally, the first day of sales ended and the employees went home tired but happy. They had found a job with a pay cheque.

Barbie's pay was $25 a week, and as soon as she saved enough she rented a room for $40 a month. In the room there was a bed, a dresser, a small table, two chairs, a hot plate, and a toaster, so that she could make some light meals. On Monday mornings Barbie put her soiled sheets, pillow cases, and towels outside the door, and the landlady would replace them with a clean set of laundry.

She spent the balance of the money on necessities. There was no money for frivolities. Since she had no refrigerator, she bought small items that could be quickly warmed on a hot plate: small tins of baked beans or spaghetti. In addition she often bought a small bag of cabbage to make coleslaw. She longed for a dish of Jello. Since the weather was getting cold she prepared some and put it outside her window on a roof to set during the night. On rare occasions she went to a little luncheon place where they specialized in inexpensive meals such as more beans or spaghetti!!

Clothes were another necessity. Since buying on credit was unknown in those days, Barbie purchased a dress or coat on the Lay-Away Plan: $5 down and $5 a payday until the purchase price was reached and the item was finally hers. When she owned adequate clothing to reach the store's high standards, she bought a teal-coloured radio—her first and most treasured possession for many years.

Barbie's great longing had been to do 'light housekeeping' for herself, but now that she was doing it she felt lonely. A friend introduced her to a Baptist Church and she enjoyed going there, but most people had belonged to little groups for years and she often felt like an outsider.

There were a couple of exceptions though. A single woman about her age asked her to come over about once a month for Sunday lunch. It consisted of bacon, eggs, and toast. It tasted so good and the company was even better. She also met a friendly, older woman named Mrs. Oliver and Barbie grew to love her. She was a bit like her mother, whom Barbie missed.

Still, the nights were long and lonely. Sometimes as she ate her meager supper in front of the only window in her room, she noticed a neighbour lady peering at her across the alley. Once for fun, Barbie waved at her, and the woman quickly looked away.

One morning Barbie woke up with a heavy cold. She realized that she needed every penny of the $100 monthly pay cheque, and if she was absent she would not be paid. So she went to work. When she arrived, the manager met her and said, "Barbara, you are sick. You must go home. If you don't, you may get pneumonia."

The old woman stopped typing and looked across the green fields as she visualized Barbie at twenty-four years old. So many years had passed and Barbie had changed. Many things were the same though: her faith, her patience, her striving to be and to do. But no, she had been different then. Because of her lameness her mother had protected her, believing that she was helping Barbie to improve. "Barbie, don't carry that. You might hurt your back. Be careful, Barbie;" and all those trips to the chiropractor. Nonsense, thought the old woman. She knew Barbie's parents had wonderful intentions but should have pushed her harder.

Sometimes when Barbie was in High School, she stayed up late and read. The next day or maybe two days later she became ill and stayed home from school. The old woman remembered how Barbie had missed a whole year of school because she hadn't felt well when it was time to enroll for a new year.

Now Barbie was all alone and sick and she made a decision. No longer was she going to be a sickly person. She decided to become healthy. She started going to bed and getting a good night's sleep instead of reading half the night. She pushed herself in a healthy way, and stood tall in her independence. But really, the old woman said to herself, I'm daydreaming too much. This should be written down instead.

The store was abuzz. Christmas shopping was in full swing and Barbie was busy. One day the Personnel Manager called the employees together, "I have something very disturbing to tell you: Some of you are shoplifting and I don't know who you are. You shame the store and your fellow employees. From now on, when you first arrive at the store you will check your purse and any bags at the Information Desk with Barbara."

The night before the store closure for the Christmas break, the manager once more called the employees together. "Sales are going to decline," she said. "The following employees are laid off from work." Then she read the names. What relief! Barbie's name was not on the list; however, the manager informed her that the Information

Desk would be closed and she was transferred to the office. There was a great deal of anger and muttering amongst the dismissed employees, and sarcastic remarks were going around: "Merry Christmas to you, too!" However, Barbie heard no more of employee stealing, and security of purses was no longer on her job description.

Barbie enjoyed office work, and when her good friend, Mrs. Oliver, told her of a more lucrative job opportunity she said, "I am very happy with my job, thank you." Life at work never seemed static.

One of her jobs was rolling coins. At the end of each day, one of the store executives came and put them all in a sack to carry them to the safe. One day the Assistant Manager grabbed the bag and threw it over his shoulders. The weight of the coins carried the bag over him backwards and fell on the floor with a thump. The end result was that Barbie and other office staff had to reroll many coins.

Another day the Personnel Manager called all the women together. Her face was red and she appeared flustered and angry. "This morning," she said, "I received a call from an office employee across the road. She said that they can't get their men to do any work because they're busy watching you women use the washroom. Why on earth would you use an uncompleted washroom stall with a window that faces the street?"

Barbie knew the story although she had never been brave enough to use that stall herself. Day after day the women had become impatient waiting for their turn at the toilets while they avoided the end stall with the window.

"I know," said one person "that's one of those new windows. You can see out but nobody can see in. Let's go, girls." (Many women believed her words although it was just plain glass!)

Barbie carried on day after day, walking down the hill to work in the mornings and climbing back up at night. She took part in church activities including Young People's meetings and when invited, Barbie spoke at another Baptist Church in the area.

Despite work and church, Barbie lived a solitary life. She had one date with a friend from Vancouver and another gentleman asked her to go to Bellingham, USA, for the weekend. She declined. She had worked less than eight months when her Dad phoned her. He said, "Barb, your mother is very ill once again. I'd like you to resign from your job and come home."

Barbie felt devastated. She loved her mother more than any other person. Immediately she resigned from her job, gave notice to the rooming house owner, packed her few belongings, and got on the train bound for Armstrong. Life was about to change but she had no idea how much.

Chapter Twelve

Home at Last

The old woman put on her shoes, went outdoors, picked up her walking stick and started out. It had been well over a year since she had started writing about Barbie and now the child's story was almost finished.

She strolled past the cow feeders. One by one each cow raised her head and looked at the old woman. What were they thinking? She didn't know. She walked on past her daughter-in-law's flower beds and through the freshly cut hay field.

On the return walk she passed the same cows as they looked at her with mournful eyes. Her husband, Martin, had left flakes of hay ready to feed, so she gave each cow and calf enough to last until he came to tend to them. She had to hurry to the house and write more about Barbie.

In the house she put on a CD of quiet reflective music, sat down at the computer, and began to type.

Once more, Barbie tended her mother until the bloom of health came into her cheeks. Offers of jobs at the coast were coming but she decided to try to find work in Armstrong where she could be near her mother in case she was needed again.

After a couple of tries at job-hunting, she was hired at the Armstrong Co-op grocery store, at a pay of $22.50 a week. She was one of two cashiers, but when there were no customers she and her co-worker Nellie stocked shelves, carried groceries out to cars, or did whatever needed to be done.

Outside the rear door stood a hitching rail to which an occasional wagon pulled by horses tied up so the driver could pick up animal feed. The store primarily carried groceries, but also animal feed and a few hardware items.

The manager, Mr. Hardy, was an interesting man. By nature he displayed a combination of strictness and compassion. Barbie respected him and tried her best to be a good employee. "Now, girls," he said, "I understand women's problems. When it is your time of the month, don't put your hands in cold water to wash the vegetables." His two female employees quietly smiled.

One day a long fluorescent ceiling light bulb erratically flashed a few times and then went out. Mr. Hardy brought out a twelve foot ladder and a new light bulb and said to Barbie, "Barbara, I want you to climb the ladder and replace the light bulb." Barbie had obeyed adults all her life, and so taking the light bulb in one hand and hanging on to the ladder with the other she started up. Partway up she looked at the height of the ceiling and estimated that she'd have to stand without support way up there to put in the bulb. Slowly, and fearing the wrath of her boss, she backed down the ladder.

"I'm sorry, Mr. Hardy. I can't do it."

"That's okay, Barbara. I knew I couldn't do it, but I thought maybe you could."

Wow, said Barbie to herself; saved by the odd traits of her boss. He might instead have asked her co-worker. Nellie was much braver, stronger, and more daring than Barbie. She carried bags of 100 pounds of flour, feed, or sugar with ease, while Barbie tackled the bags of sixty pounds. Sometimes, Nellie became hungry doing the hard work and she never hesitated to go when the boss wasn't looking and cut herself a couple of slices of baloney.

There was one customer the boss didn't like or trust. "Girls, don't talk to her." She was an old woman, who one day asked Barbie a question. Barbie answered her query. Mr. Hardy came hurrying out of his office where he had a clear view of the happenings in the store. He went straight to Barbie, "I told you not to talk to her." Barbie remained quiet and unassertive, but she felt guiltless.

One day there was a line-up of customers at Barbie's till when a tall woman walked past them until she became first in line. "Please go to the end of the line," said Barbie.

"I will not," the woman said as she raised her head and glared at Barbie, who kept on serving the people who were there before her. Finally, the lady gave her purchases to the man standing next in line who put them through the checkout. As soon as the line cleared Barbie rushed back to explain to her manager. His only comment was, "Good. She is far too bossy."

Strange, thought the old woman, but that lady met Verta one day and said to her, "I really like your daughter. She is a good cashier and has lots of spunk." Thereafter, she remained one of Barbie's greatest supporters.

One day, unnoticed by her, a stranger watched Barbie as she worked, then went back to talk to her boss.

Soon Mr Hardy approached her and said, "A stranger has been watching you work. He is an employer in a big grocery store. He said that you are a very skilful clerk, and if you ever want another job he would hire you immediately."

Still, despite the praise, Barbie knew she made mistakes. One morning a man ordered three dozen bunches of daffodils for a wedding. What a nice order, thought Barbie. So she ordered them. When the customer arrived for his order she presented what he had asked for: three dozen bunches of daffodils. "Oh, I didn't mean that many I wanted three dozen-bunches of daffodils," and that's what he took away thirty-six daffodils. Barbie looked at the tub full of daffodils, and waited for the ire of her boss. Unexpectedly, he laughed and said, "I'll take the ones that don't sell to the seniors' home. They'll enjoy them." What a surprising boss, thought Barbie.

Although work took most of her energies and by the end of the day she was tired, she decided to add other things to her life. The basement of the store where she worked held a bowling alley with an outside entrance. So along with her Dad, she joined a bowling league. She had never been a sports enthusiast, and considered herself clumsy. Whether her self-image was factual or not, she became an average bowler.

Of course, for many years she had been a faithful Christian and now she joined the local Baptist Church. The church at that time had a very active Young People's group, which Barbie promptly joined. Although the church was small, when the pastor taught the Youth Class it took up almost half the pews. Barbie became the teacher of the Young People's Sunday School class and when summer arrived she taught in the Vacation Bible School, organized and led by all the Protestant churches in Armstrong. She had always enjoyed teaching and loved the children.

Soon Barbie settled into a way of life in Armstrong. No longer did she dislike it, but still had longings for the big city. Her mother felt better and her father was busy in Terminal Motors. The three of them lived together in a two-storey house on Rosedale Avenue. Barbie walked everywhere: to work, to church, and to the bowling alley.

One day while walking past the Presbyterian Church, Barbie heard a motorcycle. Turning around, she saw her Dad driving down the quiet street on the left-hand side, as he watched the nearby lawn bowlers. Suddenly, a car came around the corner. Her father drove toward the side of the road to avoid it. Barbie watched in horror as her Dad pitched over his bike and landed on the ground. She ran down the hill where he refused her help, got on the bike, and rode to the doctor's office where he learned that he had broken his collarbone.

Yet fall was coming and change was in the air although Barbie had no inkling of what.

Chapter Thirteen

A Life Decision

The old woman sat in her lawn chair rocking back and forth in rhythm with the gentle breezes that swayed the branches of the weeping willow trees. The resident squirrel chirped its resentment of her intrusion. Blackie the cat rubbed against her leg as the old woman brushed a little bug off her writing pad. Mottled green, brown and tan grass replaced the lush green grass of spring, and the sky was misty blue from forest fires. The intense heat of summer had disappeared for the moment as nature pleaded for rain.

Life was peaceful on the farm as the old woman's mind travelled back in time to twenty-four-year-old Barbie in the little town of Armstrong.

One of Barbie's first visitors was seventeen-year-old Ann, the daughter of one of her mother's best friends. After a few friendly chats, Barbie asked Ann to spend the night with her. Bedtime came, but after they put on their pyjamas, they talked on and on into the early morning. Ann told her that her brother, Martin, had just come home from a summer working for a farmer in Alberta.

Barbie had met Martin the summer before but she had paid no attention to him, other than to note his deep blue eyes and curly brown hair. Now as Ann told story after story about her wonderful brother, Barbie became impressed. Finally Barbie's father yelled, "You girls go to sleep."

Christmas came and with it a nice card from Martin and an invitation to go out on New Year's Eve. Barbie was looking forward to the date with Martin. New Year's Eve was bitterly cold but she waited anxiously for Martin to pick her up in his Model A Ford car. As the evening wore on her young sister, Faith, teased her, "He's stood you up." Somehow that didn't seem to fit the character of the man she had heard so much about, but finally she went to bed. Her date had failed to materialize.

The old woman knew the reason. After supper on New Year's Eve Martin dressed for the big date with Barbie. He walked out the door towards his Model A and shivered. Then he picked up the crank to turn over the engine and start the car. It made a grunting noise then died. Over and over he tried and failed. He had no intention of giving up on his date night. Finally, exhausted and half frozen he stopped and went inside. He looked at the clock. "Too late to phone," he said to his Mom. "I hope Barbie will understand." Oh, the trials of young love, smiled the old woman..

Before Barbie finished work Saturday evening, Martin stood inside the door of the store waiting for her. When the store closed at nine o'clock, they went driving in the Model A. The temperature outside was still very cold, and the inside of the car was just slightly warmer, but when love happens the weather really doesn't matter.

The next Saturday night while driving in the Model A Ford, Martin proposed, and Barbie who had shown some restraint in the past threw caution to the wind and said, "Yes."

"But you'll have to wait a while," said Martin. That's okay, thought Barbie; this has happened really fast!

The next Saturday evening, January 19, 1952, after Barbie's shift they went driving in the Model A again. Martin surprised Barbie when he pulled out a golden bell-shaped box with an engagement ring in it. They didn't have to wait any longer to announce to the world that they were engaged.

At that time, her Dad was in England and her mother was in hospital in Vernon, but her sister Joyce, husband Roy, and little Linda were staying with them. Roy was overseeing the garage in Harry's absence. It was about two a.m. when Martin said "Goodbye" to Barbie at her door.

It seemed to Barbie as if she were walking on air. No one was awake in the quiet house. Linda lay in her crib, while Roy and Joyce slept soundly in the upstairs bedroom. Barbie felt like she was busting with the news and tiptoed upstairs. "Joyce, Roy: I'm engaged. I've got a ring."

"Go to bed. I know," said Joyce. "I'm tired."

Barbie's smile faded; *Well, so much for her great news.*

The next morning Joyce, Roy, and Linda accompanied Barbie to Sunday School at the church. Joyce had dressed Linda in a gorgeous blue satin dress that matched the little girl's eyes. She sat quietly in the pew, every so often walking a few steps and observing the people.

After the opening session, Barbie stood up Bible in hand, to teach the Young People's class. She did not mention her engagement. Just as she started to talk, the treasurer, a friend named Doris, came to collect the gathered donations. Barbie handed her the money and Doris' eyes opened wide when she noticed Barbie's ring. Doris, in order to get the class's attention without speaking, held out her engagement ring finger as if it were weighted down and then pointed to Barbie's left hand. The class members gasped as Barbie stumbled on with the lesson.

After lunch, Martin and Barbie traveled to Vernon Jubilee Hospital and walked up the stairs to Barbie's mother's room. "Guess what, Mom," said Barbie, as she showed Verta her ring. "We're engaged."

"I know," said her Mom, "I picked him out for you a long time ago, but I didn't dare tell you. You're so independent; I might have scared you off."

Harry received the news while visiting in England and was delighted. He had always liked Martin.

Martin's parents were pleased although his Mom declared that somehow Barbie had never seemed like a farm girl. She was more the missionary type. They decided to fix the upstairs of the farm house as an apartment for the young couple. It had never been fully finished. Ann, who was just beginning her final year of school, still occupied one room upstairs. The back bedroom was wallpapered with yellow daffodils, while the south bedroom became the new dining room and the large hall to the east was finished off as a kitchen with cupboards, a sink, a tiny fridge and a small stove. Ann painted some daffodils on the sheer kitchen curtains that matched the daffodil theme. With his $1000 savings Martin bought a new beige table with four padded seats, a double bed and dresser, and some used living room furniture.

With her savings Barbie bought a white three-quarter length wedding dress, and a pale mauve floral going-away sheer dress with matching pale mauve coat.

The wedding date was fast approaching: August 14, 1952. Martin's mother had planted a row of gladiolas that she nurtured so that they would bloom mid-August. Aunt Nellie, whose many talents included flower arrangements agreed to make all the bridal bouquets and boutonnieres for the men.

The bridesmaids were chosen. Sister Joyce, along with Roy and Linda, had gone back to Manitoba and could not return for the wedding, but Faith who had married in March of that year agreed to be her Matron of Honour, while Ann and her cousin Elaine were her bridesmaids. Martin chose his friend Jim Nelson as his Best Man, while the ushers, friend Jim Shiach and Barbie's brother, Frank, doubled as male attendants for the groom.

Dainty sandwiches and goodies were prepared by the bride and groom's mothers along with the double-layer fruit cake that was made and decorated by the bride's mother, who by now had recovered.

August 14th dawned. The day was bright and sunny. The wedding was scheduled for 2 p.m. About 1:45 p.m. Barbie and her father were dressed and ready to go to the church when they received a frantic call from the groom. All the flowers for the wedding party had been forgotten in the basement. He had to go home and get them. Barbie was calm and relaxed while her dad paced back and forth.

At the church the guests waited. The brave, young pianist, thirteen-year-old, Jeanette played the wedding hymns over again; and again. At 2:20 the wedding party started up the aisle.

Barbie's eyes were on Martin, her chosen man. He stood about five foot eight, agile and slender, with his blue eyes and curly dark brown hair. As she said her vows she had no thought of the future: of the fantastic joys and the indescribable sorrows; of poverty and good times. She just stepped into the future secure in the knowledge that God and this man would see her through.

The old woman's eyes misted with tears. She foreknew the mixed happiness of Barbie's future, but through it all Barbie would stand tall and secure in the knowledge of love. Her promise to son Jim was fulfilled. Barbie's childhood story had ended. With reluctance she laid down her pen and shut off her computer.

This book is a gift of love.

~

My love for you will never die

&

My prayers for you are forever before God.

~

Neither love nor prayers have a shelf life!